Inmates and Their Wives

INMATES AND THEIR WIVES

Incarceration and Family Life

BONNIE E. CARLSON
AND
NEIL CERVERA

Studies in Social Welfare Policies and Programs, Number 14

Greenwood Press
Westport, Connecticut • London

Library of Congress Cataloging-in-Publication Data

Carlson, Bonnie E.
  Inmates and their wives : incarceration and family life / Bonnie
E. Carlson and Neil Cervera.
      p. cm.—(Studies in social welfare policies and programs,
  ISSN 8755-5360 ; no. 14)
      Includes bibliographical references.
      ISBN 0-313-27481-9 (alk. paper)
      1. Prisoners—United States—Family relationships. 2. Prisoners'
  wives—United States. 3. Prisoners' families—United States.
  4. Social work with criminals—United States. 5. Prisoners—New
  York (State)—Family relationships—Case studies. I. Cervera,
  Neil. II. Title. III. Series.
  HV8886.U5C37   1992
  365′.6′019—dc20   92-19428

British Library Cataloguing in Publication Data is available.

Library of Congress Catalog Card Number: 92-19428
ISBN: 0-313-27481-9
ISSN: 8755-5360

First published in 1992

Greenwood Press, 88 Post Road West, Westport, CT 06881
An imprint of Greenwood Publishing Group, Inc.

Printed in the United States of America

This book is dedicated to Jean and Arnold Carlson, parents of Bonnie Carlson, who provided nurturance and support throughout the process of writing this book, and to Ellen Cervera, daughter of Neil Cervera, whose patience during the process of the project will always be remembered.

Contents

Tables

Acknowledgments

This book was conceived out of our mutual concern for incarcerated individuals and the problems they face in maintaining meaningful family ties. It would not have been possible without the support of the New York State Department of Correctional Services (NYSDOCS) and its Department of Ministerial and Family Services. We would also like to acknowledge the cooperation of the New York State correctional facilities and their staff: Great Meadow, Wallkill, Shawangunk, Sing Sing, and Washington. Specific individuals from the NYSDOCS who were instrumental in assisting us with the study were Joe Powers and Karl Gohlke. Financial support for the project was received through a Faculty Research Awards Program grant, seed money provided by the Research Foundation, State University of New York. This grant provided small amounts of support to several graduate students from the School of Social Welfare who assisted us with interviewing, coding, and data entry. These students also merit our thanks, Shao Shan Li, in particular. Finally, our heartfelt appreciation goes to the inmates and wives who shared their time, thoughts, and feelings with us and made the study possible.

Chapter 1

Introduction

This is a book about incarcerated men and their wives. It reports on a study that examines the impact of incarceration on the lives of inmates and their families and describes an innovative program in New York State that permits inmates who meet certain criteria to have extended family (conjugal) visits. The study was motivated by our recognition that family contacts may be an effective factor in minimizing future criminality in a known criminal population.

Crime has become one of the most difficult social issues confronting American society, leading to fear and changes in people's behavior. In addition, it has negative economic ramifications resulting from the reluctance of businesses to establish themselves in high-crime areas where jobs are most desperately needed (McGahey, 1988). Not surprisingly the field of corrections has become a hotly debated topic of late, in part because of the dramatic rise in the size of the incarcerated population and the associated increases in expenditures. Indeed, the situation has been described as "America's correctional crisis." This crisis has at least two dimensions: the problem of prison overcrowding and disagreement over what the objectives of incarceration should be (Gottfredson and McConville, 1987).

Between 1980 and 1984 the number of incarcerated individuals increased nationally by 41% and is rising at a faster rate than the overall increase in known crime, which has been falling slightly overall (McGahey, 1988; "U. S. Has Highest," 1991). Both the number of incarcerated persons and the rate of imprisonment are at all-time highs, with the rates being more than twice as high as any European country's (whose rates range from 35 to 120 per 100,000) and in some cases are *ten times as high* (Jorgensen et al., 1986; Netherland, 1987; "U. S. Has Highest," 1991). Since 1980, there has been a 134% increase in the size of the nation's prison population ("Inmate Population Rises," 1991). By the end of 1990, 771,243 individuals were incarcerated in state prisons according to the Bureau of Justice Statistics ("Inmate Population Rises," 1991). The 1990 rate of incarceration was 293 per 100,000, the highest it has ever been, according to the Bureau of Justice Statistics, and it now surpasses that of South Africa and the Soviet Union ("Inmate Population Rises," 1991; "U. S. Has Highest," 1991). In 1990, it was predicted by the National Council on Crime and Delinquency that between 1990 and 1993 the incarcerated population would rise by 68% to the unprecedented level of 441 per 100,000 ("Inmate Growth," 1990).

Every society has had to develop policies to deal with behavior that violates society's norms and to protect society from those who break the law. Unfortunately, there is no consensus about why people violate the law, although there is agreement that crime is a complex, costly, and multifaceted problem with behavioral, social, and economic ramifications (McGahey, 1988). The causes of criminal behavior tend to be viewed as emanating from inside the individual or within society or as an interaction between the two. Over time, there have been shifts in the extent to which individual versus societal or institutional factors have been invoked as explanations for criminality (Handler, 1975).

Beliefs about the causes of criminality and why offenders engage in criminal behavior are critically important because they influence the direction of policies and programs by affecting the assumptions that underlie them (McGahey, 1988; Thomas, 1981). In the absence of a clear consensus, even among the experts, about exactly why crime occurs, public opinion about crime and correctional policy becomes an important determinant of the kinds of policies and programs that are enacted (Gelman, 1983). In the

1980s, policymakers have been observed to "often have an extreme vision of what the public and other political actors demand," creating incorrect assumptions that result in more conservative decisions about correctional policy than might otherwise be made (McGahey, 1988, 550).

Perhaps because of this lack of consensus about the causes of crime because of its enormous complexity, there is no single, unitary policy that governs the corrections field in this country. Rather, there is a complex amalgam of different and sometimes conflicting policies enacted at the federal, state, and local levels, derived through negotiation and compromise among different interest groups, which ultimately determines what happens in our prison system (Gelman, 1983).

This package of policies has created a correctional system in the United States that has been described as "amorphous, difficult to understand, and costly. It appears to be a fluid, flexible system that is constantly changing, but it is rigid and intractable, a system that has not significantly changed since its inception" (Netherland, 1987, 351). How has the correctional system gotten to this point? To understand the system that has evolved to deal with our most persistent and serious offenders it may be helpful to present a brief history of the American correctional system.

HISTORICAL UNDERPINNINGS OF AMERICAN CORRECTIONS

Even before the United States was colonized, the traditions that were to form the basis for our correctional system were being established. As far back as the Middle Ages in Europe, when torture, fines, and corporal punishment were employed as the primary means of dealing with criminal offenders and the Church was more heavily involved in addressing criminal behavior than the state, the values of punishment and retribution prevailed. Eventually the state wrested control over the offending population from the Church. However, the strong belief in punishment established during the Middle Ages was exported to the United States with the early colonists, influencing American correctional policy to this day (Garland, 1990; Rothman, 1971; Sherman and Hawkins, 1981).

Another common correctional practice to emerge at the time of colonization was that of banishing the offender from the community to faraway places, such as the United States and Australia (Hatcher, 1978). Indeed, Australia was first settled as a penal colony. Remnants of this policy are evident today in the practice of placing offenders in distant facilities, typically in rural areas far from their home communities. Although it is widely recognized that this practice is rarely in the best interest of offenders, it often accomplishes another goal, that of providing jobs and resources in poor rural areas where unemployment is often high (Nagel, 1973).

By the early 1900s a change in orientation had occurred in which criminals were to be sent to prison *as* punishment rather than *for* punishment. Work was still the major thrust of the correctional approach, but corporal punishment began to be de-emphasized, and more prisons were initiating educational programs (Hatcher, 1978).

The first evidence of rehabilitation (as we know it today) in modern correctional facilities appeared in the form of social casework, first introduced by the Federal Bureau of Prisons. This innovation occurred as a result of reforms following problems associated with overcrowding, insufficient staffing, and rioting during the Depression. The Bureau of Prisons, under the jurisdiction of the Department of Justice, was reorganized and hired a new group of college-educated professionals who were reform-minded and believed that societal conditions, such as poverty, caused crime.

At about this same time the modern version of *classification*, the system by which inmates are assigned to different programs matched with their specific needs, emerged. As prison riots and control problems continued through the 1950s, concerns mounted about the conditions of correctional facilities and the way inmates were treated, leading to even greater emphasis on the classification system and louder cries for more humanitarian treatment (Hatcher, 1978).

PHILOSOPHY AND GOALS OF CONTEMPORARY CORRECTIONS

In more modern times criminal justice and correctional policy has been informed by three overarching objectives: community safety, fiscal responsibility and policy effectiveness, and equity and justice (McGahey, 1988). Oftentimes, the objectives of societal protection, fiscal responsibility, and policy effectiveness (operationalized in part as offender rehabilitation) conflict with one another and must be reconciled (Gelman, 1983).

The correctional system has emphasized a variety of different justifications or goals for its programs. These include (1) *retribution* (punishment) or imposition of unpleasant consequences on the offender that are intended to uphold the moral order of society; (2) restraint or *incapacitation* of the offender, that is, removing him from the community to prevent commission of crimes during the period of the sentence; (3) *general deterrence* of future criminality by imposition of sanctions on offenders; (4) *specific deterrence* of future criminal behavior by a particular offender; and (5) *rehabilitation* of the offender through planned interventions that are nonintimidative (Balogh, 1964; Duffee, 1989; Gelman, 1983; Gottfredson and Taylor, 1987; McGahey, 1988; Netherland, 1987; Spiro, 1978; Thomas, 1981).

Although the late 1950s and 1960s saw a shift in focus away from the other goals toward an emphasis on rehabilitation of the offender (Handler, 1975; Zemans and Cavan, 1958), a growing pessimism about the success of rehabilitation efforts in corrections as well as the deterrent value of incarceration developed in the 1970s. The pessimism about rehabilitation is perhaps understandable in light of recidivism rates that have continued at an unacceptably high level going back at least to the 1960s. Recidivism is high despite a substantial shift in approach away from retribution and punishment and in favor of intervention, treatment, and programming as the means of changing the offender in the hopes that he will refrain from criminal behavior in the future.

This pessimism was embodied in the so-called "Martinson Report," a review of over 200 studies of various types of community-based and institutional correctional interventions (Martinson, 1974). The interventions studied ranged from probation and parole to educational programming, individual and group psychotherapy, milieu therapy, and casework. The outcome measures investigated included not only recidivism rates but also institutional and vocational adjustment, educational achievement, personality and attitudinal change, and community adjustment. The overall conclusion was that "with few and isolated exceptions, the rehabilitation efforts that have been reported so far have had no appreciable effect on recidivism" (Martinson, 1974, 25). However, the Martinson report did not investigate the effects on recidivism of family visits or other family-based interventions, which are the subject of this study.

Nonetheless, despite the fact that Martinson himself later repudiated the report, it was influential, and the pendulum shifted away from emphasis on rehabilitation and back to more punitive approaches. Since the beginning of the 1980s the main value of corrections is seen to be its ability to punish and incapacitate offenders (McGahey, 1988; Spiro, 1978; Thomas, 1981). While this approach keeps some of the worst criminals off the streets and may deter some from committing crimes, thereby protecting the community, it does nothing to modify the conditions that led to criminal behavior, either within the individual or within society. The 1980s have witnessed an unprecedented trend toward prison expansion as the major means of dealing with a rapidly expanding offender population that increasingly has drug problems. When prison is viewed as the primary means of protecting society, costs are guaranteed to rise dramatically, as has been the case for the 1980s, as is discussed later (McGahey, 1988).

But there are indications that those who influence correctional policy have had "liberal" attitudes favoring rehabilitation as far back as the early 1970s and that these attitudes continue into the present, while the policymakers significantly misperceive the attitudes of the general public. At least three research studies comparing attitudes toward corrections held by policymakers and the general public in several states have identified discrepancies wherein liberal-leaning, rehabilitation-oriented policymakers perceived the public to be significantly more conservative and punitive in their orientation than they actually were (Gottfredson and Taylor, 1987). Correcting such misperceptions is critically important to being able to forge correctional policies that are forward-thinking and supported by a majority of the public.

As the number of new drug-related commitments rises, there is renewed interest in rehabilitation at the federal level and in several states including New York, based on the need for substance abuse treatment. On the federal level, 45% of inmates are said to have histories of substance abuse, a 5% increase over past years and perhaps double the rate of a decade ago. A multifaceted strategy involves (1) the designation of several comprehensive treatment centers scattered around the country; (2) the development of "high-intensity" pilot programs involving continuous treatment in three facilities; and (3) the establishment of drug counseling programs at all federal facilities, with a mandated drug education program for all inmates with a history of drug abuse, as well as aftercare services for released offenders. However, there is controversy over how such programs can be funded ("Drug Programs," 1990).

CHARACTERISTICS OF THE INCARCERATED POPULATION

Probably the most noteworthy characteristic of the current prison population is its rapidly increasing size. As of 1988 there were 603,732 inmates in state and federal correctional facilities (Flanagan and Maguire, 1990). The 1987 rate of incarceration was 228 per 100,000, which rose to 244 a year later and to 426 per 100,000 by 1990. However, these national rates are averages across the fifty states. The 1988 rate of 244 reflects widely varying rates ranging from a low of 62 per 100,000 in North Dakota to highs of over 300 per 100,000 in states such as Alaska, South

Carolina, Louisiana, and Delaware. Nevada's incarceration rate in 1988 was 452 per 100,000 (Flanagan and Maguire, 1990). The rate in New York, the state in which this study was performed, was 248 in 1988, just about the national average. It is important to keep in mind that as the rate of incarceration rises, so does the number of significant others, mostly family members—wives, children, mothers, and fathers—who are indirectly affected by imprisonment of an offender.

An important issue concerns the reasons for the rapid rise in the size of the incarcerated population. One obvious factor might be the overall crime rate, except that it has stabilized in most categories, except drug-related crime, which has risen dramatically. "Drug-related crime is [said to be] the biggest cause of the increase in the prison population" according to the Sentencing Project, a research group ("U. S. Has Highest," 1991). In addition, four other factors have converged to explain the rise in incarcerated offenders: a "tougher court and prosecutorial climate"; the full implementation of new laws mandating prison sentences for certain crimes, such as drug trafficking and the possession of guns, as well as mandatory prison sentences for second felonies; determinate sentences for certain crimes; and a trend toward assignment of longer sentences, especially for violent offenders and recidivists (McGahey, 1988; Rogers, 1989).

The incarcerated population continues to be overwhelmingly male (96%) and young; 27% of incarcerated offenders are less than twenty-five years of age, and only 26% are thirty-five years of age or older (Jamieson and Flanagan, 1989). Another noteworthy characteristic is the extent to which nonwhites are overrepresented in the incarcerated population. At the federal level, 66% of inmates are white, whereas at the state level only 48% are white; the remainder are nonwhite, overwhelmingly black and Latino. The federal, state, and local incarceration rate for black males is 3,109 per 100,000, in contrast to 426 per 100,000 overall ("U. S. Has Highest," 1991). The degree of minority overrepresentation is greatest in the South and least pronounced in the West (Jamieson and Flanagan, 1989).

Inmates are also noted for their limited educational backgrounds and low levels of prearrest employment. As of 1986 almost two-thirds of state prisoners had not completed high school, and only 57% were employed full-time at the time of arrest; another 12% were employed on a part-time basis prior to incarceration. Although about one-third were not employed at the time of their arrest, almost half of those were not even looking for employment (Jamieson and Flanagan, 1989).

Regarding their marital status, only 20% of prisoners at the state level were married at the time of their incarceration, although another 23% were separated or divorced. Thus, over half of the inmate population has not been legally married, in part attributable to their young age (Jamieson and Flanagan, 1989). Many of those who are not legally married are in common-law relationships. Among federal prisoners, as of 1989 34% were married, 22% were separated or divorced, and 8% were in common-law relationships (Flanagan and Maguire, 1990). However, despite this distribution of marital status, most inmates probably have dependent children as a result of their current or past legal marriages or through a common-law union (Hairston, 1990). This fact has important ramifications for the overall impact of incarceration on inmates themselves as well as the larger community from which they come.

Also noteworthy is the extent to which substance abuse is associated with incarceration. Based on 1986 statistics, it is estimated that over one-third of inmates were under the influence of illegal drugs at the time of their current offense; another 19% were estimated to have been under the influence of alcohol while committing the crime for which they are currently confined. An even larger number were estimated to have used drugs daily in the month preceding their current offense. However, only 8.4% of those in state prisons were convicted of drug offenses, most often drug trafficking (Jamieson and Flanagan, 1989).

Most inmates will serve relatively brief sentences in correctional facilities. Although the average sentence length was sixty-five months in 1984, only 45% of that sentence is likely to have been served in prison on average, which amounts to just under two years served in jail and prison. Thus, not only will the vast majority of incarcerated offenders be returned to the community, but they will be returned after relatively brief stays in correctional facilities.

A minority, or 18.5%, of those currently incarcerated are serving a first sentence. The remainder are recidivists, having been returned to prison for commission of a new offense or for a probation or parole violation committed while a youthful or adult offender. As mentioned previously, recidivism continues at a high level. Estimates made by the Bureau of Justice Statistics for inmates released in 1983 across eleven states that account for over half of the total incarcerated population (California, Florida, Illinois, Michigan, Minnesota, New Jersey, New York, North Carolina, Ohio, Oregon, and Texas) indicate that 63% of released offenders will be arrested in the first three years following their release. Almost half will be convicted of a new crime, and 41% will be returned to prison by the end of that period (Jamieson and Flanagan, 1989).

Because of the scope of the crime problem and specifically the number of incarcerated individuals, enormous increases in societal resources have been allocated to this problem, resources that might of course be spent in other ways (Gottfredson & McConville, 1987). During 1989 and 1990, $8.4 billion was authorized nationally to be spent on construction of new prison cells alone (Malcolm, 1990).

In 1986 almost $16 billion was spent by all levels of government on criminal justice activities. Approximately two-thirds of the total was expended by the states as opposed to federal or local governments (Jamieson and Flanagan, 1989). About half of the combined criminal justice monies at the state and local levels were spent on police protection, and just under one-third was expended for correctional programs. However, at the state level over half of the total criminal justice dollars were spent on corrections. Perhaps more important was the fact that the proportion of total criminal justice expenditures allocated to corrections was rising faster than any other category of criminal justice expenditure.

It is also illuminating to examine how money is allocated at the state level within the corrections field, where it can be spent on institutional corrections or alternative programs. Overwhemingly, states have chosen to allocate the lion's share of their correctional dollars to institutional programs (in part because institutional programs are so much more costly than noninstitutional programs), despite the fact that the vast majority of offenders are in community-based programs.

On the federal level, the picture is quite different. Over half of the federal dollars in 1988–1990 were spent on law enforcement, whereas only 10–14% was spent on corrections. However, the overall trend is similar to that at the state level in that the proportion of dollars allocated for correctional programs is steadily rising (Jamieson and Flanagan, 1989).

SUMMARY AND CONCLUSIONS

The American corrections field has undergone many changes since colonial times. In some respects the field can be said to have come full circle insofar as retribution was the primary goal in the beginning and after many changes in orientation has once again become the overarching purpose of imprisonment, in conjunction with incapacitation. The size of the incarcerated population has skyrocketed, and recidivism remains at a high level, perpetuating a state of recurrent correctional crisis. The public is outraged at the extent and the effects of the crime problem, especially in our largest cities where drugs, weapons, and violence are rampant. If there was ever a sense of optimism about our ability to solve the problem of crime in America, it has been replaced by "confusion and disagreement over the objectives and effectiveness of correctional treatment" (Gottfredson and McConville, 1987, 3).

However, some states are beginning to recognize that there is a limit to the extent to which taxpayers can be asked to assume the enormous costs of building more and more prisons and incarcerating more and more inmates. One obvious strategy is to explore more seriously community-based alternatives, which for certain categories of offenders are no less effective in deterring future crime and are much less costly. Michigan, Georgia, and Virginia have begun to actively pursue such alternatives, despite the fears of many politicians of being perceived as "soft on crime" (Thomas, 1990). But in the meantime, a vast number of individuals remain locked away in correctional facilities, separated from their families and communities, paying their debt to society. How we choose to treat them will influence how we are judged as a society. Spiro (1978) has commented that:

> In a civilized, democratic society the *sine qua non* of a criminal justice system is the just and equitable treatment of criminal offenders in which sanctions are imposed by the most humanitarian means consistent with the goal of protecting the community (319).

We can decide that retribution and incapacitation will be our primary correctional strategies, but they come with certain costs. The most obvious cost is economic. But another cost—less obvious, more indirect, and more difficult to measure—lies in the fact that when we incarcerate inmates primarily for retribution, we punish their families as well (Kiersh, 1979; Showalter and Jones, 1980). It is this effect of imprisonment that inspired us to undertake the research described in this book.

THE RESEARCH STUDY

An interest in the families of offenders as well as family-based programming for offenders led to the research described herein. We were fortunate to be in one of the few states with a program allowing so-called conjugal visits and were interested in learning more about their impact on the male inmate and his family, something that had not yet been systematically investigated. In addition, we wanted to learn more about the effects of incarceration on marital functioning. Supported by a very limited literature, common sense suggested the conclusion that incarceration was a major source of stress on couple relationships, with many dissolving in the early stages of imprisonment. But many other marriages survived incarceration, and we wanted to understand how and why.

Accordingly, we set out to learn more about extended family visits between New York State inmates and their wives who participated in the Family Reunion Program (FRP). We hoped to learn what happened during a typical visit, beyond the sexual interaction for which such visits have become famous—or infamous—but also to understand how such visits were perceived by participating family members. On the one hand, we expected that these visits would be enjoyable and eagerly anticipated. But we also recognized the possibility of awkwardness, discomfort, tension, or conflict between a couple who do not have the opportunity to see one another frequently and who may have been physically separated for as long as several years.

We were also interested in learning more about how the wives of inmates, the other victims of crime, function and cope during a husband's incarceration, and in particular the extent to which they rely on support from significant others, especially family members.

In Chapter 2, literature will be reviewed pertaining to the effect of incarceration on inmates and their families and the importance of family visits to the current and future well-being of inmates. Chapter 3 describes the research questions that were investigated as well as the methods and procedures used to conduct the study. The characteristics of the inmates and wives who were studied are also described. In Chapters 4, 5, and 6 the findings of the research are presented and discussed. Chapters 7 and 8 address the relevant policy and program implications that emerged from our findings, as well as detailed ideas for those wishing to work clinically or therapeutically with inmates and their wives. Finally, Chapter 9 summarizes the major findings and presents ideas for future research on inmate family relationships.

Chapter 2

The Literature on Incarceration and Family Life

INTRODUCTION

Each year incarceration causes many women to lose a husband or son and children to lose their fathers temporarily to imprisonment. Unlike other forms of time-limited family separation, such as a husband being away in the military, the family dismemberment caused by incarceration tends to be accompanied by stigma and demoralization (Hill, 1965). Relatively little attention has been paid to this phenomenon. Significant others, especially wives, parents, and children of criminal offenders, have been largely neglected by both researchers and service providers (Fishman and Alissi, 1979; Hinds, 1981; Kiser, 1991).

Families of offenders have been called the "hidden victims of crime" (Bakker et al., 1978). Although the inmate is separated from his family, in most cases only temporarily, the influence of the family can still be quite salient. Many inmates have less than ideal family relationships with parents, spouses, and children before they are incarcerated, making it difficult to engage the family once imprisonment occurs. However, if the offender and family can become reinvolved, through visits and other forms of contact, family ties can be rekindled and used in a rehabilitative manner to assist the inmate to make the kinds of changes necessary for future reintegration into the community (Glaser, 1964; Ingram and Swartzfager, 1973).

This chapter reviews what is known about stress and crisis and their impact on families, and specifically the effects of incarceration on the offender and his family. In addition, there is a discussion of how offenders and families cope with incarceration and the stress it imposes, with special attention devoted to the role of visiting, in particular conjugal visits.

FAMILY STRESS, CRISIS, AND COPING

Models of family stress and coping were originally developed in the 1940s. Hill's (1965) classic ABCX model of family stress was relatively simple. A stressor event (A) was said to interact with the resources a family had to meet a crisis (B) and the family's subjective definiton of the event (C), to produce X, a crisis characterized by a certain degree of family disruption. This model has helped us to understand why the same stressor events can produce varying reactions in different families.

Research on family stress and coping has addressed the factors influencing whether or not a stressor event becomes a full-blown crisis for a family and how much disorganization is experienced, as well as the postcrisis variables affecting family adaptation or recovery from stress, what has been called the family's "regenerative power" (Burr, 1973). We have learned a great deal about how families cope with stressful events since the 1950s, and Hill's original model has been elaborated on by others. Several different clusters of variables have been found to influence whether or not a stressor becomes a crisis, as well as the reorganization or recovery process. These include characteristics of the stressor event itself, the context in which the family is functioning, the quality of family functioning prior to the onset of the stressor event, and the family's history.

The A Factor: The Stressor Event

Hill (1965) originally defined a stressor as "a situation for which the family has had little or no prior preparation" (34). In contrast,

Burr (1973) has defined a stressor event as "an event that produces a change in the family social system [such as its] boundaries, structure, goals, processes, roles or values" (201). We prefer the Burr definition insofar as certain stressors, such as incarceration of a husband, almost invariably disrupt a family's functioning and create a crisis for most offenders, irrespective of previous experience (Cobean and Power, 1978). However, one British study did not find a husband's incarceration to be an inevitable crisis for all families (Morris, 1965).

Stressor events vary across a number of different dimensions, such as the degree of hardship associated with them. Hardship is an attribute of the event itself, rather than how it is perceived (Hill, 1965; McCubbin and McCubbin, 1987), and it can be defined as "those complications in a crisis-producing event which demand competencies from the family" (Hill, 1965, 35).

Three salient dimensions have been identified across which stressor events can vary: source, effect on family configuration, and type of event (Hill, 1965). Stressor events can originate in the environment external to the family, such as a war or natural disaster, or internal to the family, for example an illegitimate pregnancy or alcoholism. In general, externally originating stressor events are more easily assimilated by a family because they are frequently common to many families. In addition, when blame for the event can be placed externally, the event may actually have a solidifying rather than disorganizing effect.

In terms of family structure, many stressor events involve changes in membership, that is dismemberment (loss of a member) or accession (gain of a member), which may be accompanied by demoralization, or loss of morale or family unity. According to Hill (1965), most crises of dismemberment, of which incarceration is an example, eventually lead to demoralization.

Finally, Hill identifies two different types of stressors: those involving a change in family status and those involving conflict among members over their respective roles. Again, incarceration has implications for both types insofar as its stigmatizing nature typically means a decrease in family status, and it almost inevitably leads to significant changes in and possible conflict about family roles.

Other dimensions are relevant as well. For example, some stressors are rapid onset and acute in nature, while others, like incarceration, are slower to occur but are chronic and long-term in nature. Because of the properties of our criminal justice system, the time from arrest, through arraignment, trial and sentencing, and imprisonment is often quite long. This almost ensures that the family begins to experience the debilitating effects of stress well before incarceration actually occurs. This also means that by the time incarceration finally takes place, the family's functioning may have already deteriorated.

Stressor events vary in other ways as well. Some are viewed universally with great sympathy, such as the death of a child, while others are very stigmatizing, like learning that you have AIDS or are being sent to prison. Although a certain amount of ambiguity is inherent in most crises, some stressor events are characterized by high degrees of intrafamily or social ambiguity. This uncertainty can raise questions about the family's structure, boundaries, roles, or rules (McCubbin and McCubbin, 1987). For example, imprisonment of the husband/father may lead to questions such as: Should the marriage continue? Is the inmate still a member of the family? Who is in charge of the family? And, who should be told of the incarceration? Finally, certain stressor events can be eliminated, such as alcoholism, whereas others, like incarceration, can only be accommodated.

The B Factor: Resources

A family's resources are tremendously valuable in helping them to prevent a stressful event from disrupting the family to the point where it becomes a crisis. Three broad types of resources can be identified: personal, family system, and community. Personal resources consist of strengths of individual family members, such as high intelligence or self-esteem or a sense of personal mastery. Family system resources include such things as good communication, consensus by family members on roles and rules, and high cohesiveness. Community resources refer to formal social agencies and services, but they also include social support from close friends and more distant acquaintances. Communities vary considerably in how adequate their resources are in terms of supporting families who are attempting to cope with stressful life events (McCubbin and McCubbin, 1987).

Another way of thinking about this factor is in terms of family vulnerability (Hansen, 1965). A theoretical reformulation has identified family vulnerability as a separate factor (V), which consists of the pile-up of demands on the family in conjunction with its life cycle stage (McCubbin and McCubbin, 1987). Pile-up is more likely to occur when the stressor event is a chronic, long-term one, such as incarceration, rather than a short-term problem. Certain family life cycle stages, such as when children are very young, as is the case for many prison families, are also associated with higher degrees of family vulnerability. In addition, prior strains exist in most families as carryovers from previous unresolved hardships and can magnify the degree of hardship associated with a stressor event. Poverty, for example, or the stress associated with an arrest and trial, or substance abuse, may be prior strains in families ultimately faced with incarceration.

The C Factor: Family Appraisal

A family's appraisal or subjective definition of a stressor event is critical in influencing how they will respond to it and whether or not it will become a crisis. A family's definition of a stressor event is influenced not only by objective aspects of the event, as discussed previously, but also by its values. In addition, such appraisals will be affected by previous experiences with crisis, as well as community standards and values about the particular stressor event they are experiencing (Hill, 1965). For example, incarceration of a middle-class father who had been employed may be viewed as more disruptive by his family than imprisonment of a lower-class father, who had been unemployed and, therefore, was not contributing to the family economically.

Another dimension of the C factor pertains to family attributions about the stressor event. The source of the event, as discussed earlier, is important and may affect attributions about it. When the origin of an event is internal to the family and is perceived as being caused by a family member, that person tends to be devalued. In contrast, if the source of the event is external, or if blame is externalized, the family member's status can be preserved (Hill, 1965). In the case of incarceration, it is relevant to ask if the husband/father himself is held responsible for his criminal act, or whether blame is externalized to factors such as the availability and temptation of drugs, persecution by the police, or being in the wrong place at the wrong time.

Factors Influencing Postcrisis Reorganization or Recovery

As early as 1964 Hill and Hansen had begun to articulate some of the factors that affect the process of recovering from a crisis, virtually all of which are closely related to factors that influence whether or not a stressor event becomes a crisis. Specifically, Hansen and Hill (1964) identified (1) the suddenness of the onset of the stressor event; (2) whether the family is an extended or nuclear type; (3) affectional patterns and marital adjustment; (4) how power is exercised within the family, with a "family council type of decision-making" being most adaptive; (5) social involvement outside of the family by the wife; and (6) previous successful experience with crisis, due to the possibility of anticipatory socialization.

Other factors have also been identified as facilitating healthy family reorganization and recovery from a crisis. These include high family cohesion ("bonds of coherence and unity running through family life") and adaptability ("the ability of a family to change its structure or way of operating with little psychic or organizational discomfort") (Angell, 1936, 144). McCubbin and

McCubbin (1987) also identified cohesive and adaptable families as better able to recover from a crisis.

Quality of coping will also strongly influence family adaptation to stressful events. Family stress creates a state of tension when a family perceives an imbalance between the demands arising from a stressor event and its capacity to meet those demands (McCubbin and McCubbin, 1987). Coping behaviors help to restore the balance between demands arising from the stressor event and family resources by (1) reducing those demands, (2) acquiring new resources, (3) reallocating existing resources, (4) managing the tensions created by the imbalance, or (5) redefining the situation so as to make it more manageable. A coping behavior has been defined as "a specific effort (covert or overt) by which an individual (or group of individuals such as the family) attempts to reduce or manage a demand on the family system" (McCubbin and McCubbin, 1987, 22).

Three general types of coping strategies have been identified: avoidance, elimination, and assimilation. In *avoidance* the family denies the existence of the stressful event or simply ignores the problem in the hope that it will go away. *Elimination* involves active family efforts to change or remove the stressor event or to alter its definition of the event. *Assimilation* entails accepting the demands arising from the event into the existing family structure and process while making few if any changes in how the family operates (McCubbin and McCubbin, 1987). In the case of incarceration, assimilation is likely to be the most adaptive coping strategy, although altering how incarceration is defined may also have adaptive aspects.

Summary

A model of family stress, crisis, and reorganization has been introduced to provide a framework for understanding the responses and experiences of incarcerated husbands and their wives. The works of Hill (1965), Burr (1973), and McCubbin and McCubbin (1987) have been used to identify the critical elements that must be taken into account to understand how families are affected by the imprisonment of a member.

To understand family responses to incarceration we must consider properties of the stressor event itself (A); the family's preexisting vulnerabilities, as well as strengths or resources (B); and how the family subjectively perceives and defines incarceration, and whom they hold responsible for it (C). In addition, their recovery from or reorganization following incarceration will be influenced by many of these same factors, as well as the type and quality of coping behaviors they use to stabilize the situation. With this discussion as a background, the specific effects of incarceration on families, couples, and individual family members will be considered next.

EFFECTS ON THE FAMILY SYSTEM

Incarceration has a number of effects on the family system as a whole. Any type of dismemberment necessitates family readjustment, but when it is accompanied by stigma, shame, and embarrassment the task of achieving a new equilibrium is more complicated (Fishman, 1990; Hannon et al., 1984). The stigma accompanying incarceration affects the whole family, leading some members to distance themselves overtly or covertly from the offender by not visiting or communicating in other ways or, in the extreme, through divorce (Brodsky, 1975; Ingram and Swartzfager, 1973). Thus, separation from the offender constitutes at least a temporary emotional crisis for most families (Freedman and Rice, 1977; Scott, 1983). In that sense, incarceration punishes the family as well as the inmate (Schneller, 1976).

At the very least, family adjustment to imprisonment necessitates role changes, wherein the roles previously performed by the inmate must be reassigned to someone else, usually the wife. And yet, the inmate is not totally out of the family, and may attempt to retain control of some aspects of family life (Fishman, 1990), leading to a situation where "the inmate may still be attempting to continue the role of the head of the family *in absentia*, while losing touch with the day-to-day realities" (Jorgensen et al., 1986, 48). Thus, the family must come to terms with both excluding and including the absent husband and father (Fishman, 1990; Hannon et al., 1984). This can be even more difficult than completely losing the family member altogether, as is the case when a spouse dies.

The marital subsystem—the husband and wife dyad—is severely affected by incarceration of the husband. Many of these marriages were seriously stressed prior to incarceration due to the husband's criminal activities and/or substance abuse, and poverty, or for other reasons (Fishman, 1990; Morris, 1965). Imprisonment tends to exacerbate preexisting problems and, in addition, creates marital tension and an additional set of complex problems (Marsh, 1983; Showalter and Hunsinger, 1985).

Most importantly, the conditions and constraints of prison life make it extremely difficult to maintain a marriage (Howlett, 1973; Showalter and Hunsinger, 1985). Specifically, there are limited opportunities for contact or communication of any sort, much less intimate verbal or physical communication or shared activities (Howlett, 1973). This problem is most severe for long-term inmates. A wife and family may be willing to wait two or three years, the length of an average sentence, although even a sentence of that length is extremely disruptive and difficult for those on the outside. However, a sentence of fifteen or twenty years may create barriers that make it virtually impossible for a marriage to survive (Crosthwaite, 1975; Flanagan, 1981).

The findings of Holt and Miller's (1972) study of California inmates support this conclusion. They found that marital contacts tended to decrease over the course of an inmate's term beginning in the second year, in contrast to contacts with others, which were maintained. After the third year of incarceration, one-quarter or fewer of wives were still visiting, suggesting marital deterioration. Visiting by common-law wives occurred even less frequently. The authors interpret the cause of this marital deterioration to be the inability of the offender to reciprocate, in the context of a voluntary relationship where mutuality and reciprocation are critical (Holt and Miller, 1972).

Oftentimes inmates have trouble understanding how difficult it is for those on the outside. They expect their wives to provide both practical and emotional support to them, which severely taxes families that may only be functioning at a marginal level. In order to accomplish this, the family system must reorganize both when incarceration occurs and then again when the offender is released. This means that the wife must learn to assume the roles of husband and father as well as wife and mother, and then must be able to relinquish the new roles once the inmate returns (Ekland-Olson et al., 1983).

A related factor that impinges on marital adjustment pertains to the wives' newfound autonomy. Although effective adaptation of wives necessitates learning how to survive independently from their spouses, their husbands may become jealous and feel threatened by their wife's ability to be competent and self-sufficient without them (Showalter and Jones, 1980).

In light of the many threats to the marital subsystem, it is interesting that some marriages respond to these circumstances by improving—becoming closer and healthier—although the majority respond by deteriorating, an observation made by several authors who have studied inmate marital relationships over time (Brodsky, 1975; Fishman, 1990; Hannon et al., 1984; Freedman and Rice, 1977). Perhaps the variability in impact is accounted for by Hill's (1965) observation that family relations are solidified when blame for a stress event is externalized, which occurs in some but not all prison families.

The final way in which the family system is affected by incarceration is economic. Given that most inmates come from families that are poor to begin with, the loss of a member who contributed income, whether obtained legally or illegally, creates financial difficulties for the family (Fishman, 1990; Hinds, 1981; Pueschel and Moglia, 1977; Schneller, 1975b; Swan, 1981). Loss of the breadwinner to incarceration may mean that the wife must enter the job market, often without marketable skills or the ability to earn an income adequate to support her family alone, or to resort to public assistance. Only in the situation where the offender was both unemployed and not contributing income in any other way would the family's economic situation remain relatively the same before and after incarceration.

To summarize, the experience of incarceration tends to place major burdens on the family system. The stigma associated with incarceration and the need to offer practical, emotional, and financial support to the inmate leads to stress and often economic difficulties for family members. The marital unit is most severely affected insofar as the conditions of prison life impose serious barriers to the maintainance of marital ties, although some couples manage to overcome these obstacles and actually strengthen their relationships.

Effects on Inmates

Imprisonment has a profound impact on an inmate's sense of well-being, potentially leading to numerous psychological problems. The emotional difficulties include loneliness, guilt, self-blame, anxiety, depression, loss of sleep, diminished appetite, and feelings of powerlessness and hopelessness (Cobean and Power, 1978; Freedman and Rice, 1977; Rieger, 1973; Showalter and Hunsinger, 1985). These psychological reactions are related to the loss of family, friends, and community in the world beyond the prison walls and are associated with adjustment to prison life.

Prison is a hostile environment that fosters and encourages dependency and distrust of other inmates and prison personnel, restricts choices, and offers limited options for decision making and problem solving (Showalter and Hunsinger, 1985). These conditions, along with the lack of safety and trust, can contribute to the inmate's anger, hyperaggressiveness, or apathy.

For most inmates, separation from and loss of direct contact with their family, wife or girlfriend, and children causes distress, worry, and feelings of loss or depression (Lanier, 1987). In addition, a deterioration of the inmate's self-image can contribute to low expectations of marriage and a belief that a poor relationship is normal (Hannon et al., 1984). Inmates, especially first-timers and those who are newly married, may also have difficulty believing that their wives will remain sexually faithful to them (Howlett, 1973). These psychological reactions to family loss may undermine the inmate's ability to cope in a hostile environment and refrain from future criminal activity on his release from prison (Hairston, 1988; Howser and MacDonald, 1982).

Three stages have been observed in inmates' reactions to the loss of their families during imprisonment. During the first few weeks of incarceration the inmate faces the knowledge that he will be imprisoned for a long stay. He copes with this through escape fantasies, where he sees himself escaping back home to his family and friends. When running away from prison is recognized as being unrealistic, anxiety and depression set in (Cobean and Power, 1978).

During the middle stage of incarceration the inmate focuses on the realities of prison life. Some inmates become enraged, using belligerent behavior as a means of psychological displacement of their anger onto other inmates or staff (Cobean and Power, 1978). Older and long-term inmates have been found to be less likely to use fighting or other inappropriate behaviors, serving time to their own best advantage (Flanagan, 1981). Some inmates acquire "a prisoner identity," taking on the dysfunctional mannerisms, attitudes, and behaviors of professional criminals (Brodsky, 1975; Hannon et al., 1984). This identity may mask underlying difficulties such as financial, emotional, or psychological problems at home (Cobean and Power, 1978). During this stage, the visits to the correctional facility may be experienced as degrading and emotionally painful for both the inmate and his family (Cobean and Power, 1978).

In the final stage of incarceration, the anticipated release from the correctional institution is met with mixed feelings. First, there is a sense of grief and loss related to leaving friends and a predictable environment. While there are positive feelings, there is also anxiety and fear about what may or may not be awaiting them from family and friends (Cobean and Power, 1978).

Traditionally, prisoners have used letter writing and visits as a means of maintaining relationships with their family and friends, to show concern about their welfare, and as a way of coping with despair (Brodsky, 1975). It is important for an inmate to believe that his family is waiting for him to be released in order to have hope for the future and avoid despair (Showalter and Jones, 1980). Loss of his relationship with his family leaves an inmate bereft of significant attachments to the outside world, leading to a loss of positive feelings about himself. Thus, those prisoners who succeed in maintaining their links with their families are less likely to assume a prisoner identity (Brodsky, 1975; Hannon et al., 1984).

Sometimes the stress of incarceration causes inmates to become highly dependent on family members for their emotional needs. An inmate's dependency on his marriage may be so great that it leads to idealization of the relationship and denial of the existence of problems (Showalter and Jones, 1985). As a result, many inmates with troubled relationships perceive their marriages to be satisfactory, a belief that may be based more on wishful thinking than on reality (Morris, 1965).

Sometimes family members, dissatisfied with their relationship with the inmate, may react by withdrawing from the relationship. In addition, subsequent arrests and convictions increase stigma, making family members even more reluctant to remain involved or inducing them to sever contact with the prisoner altogether (Holt and Miller, 1972). As a result of these discrepancies in perceptions, the inmate may be unprepared to cope with the breakup of the relationship and he may experience a personal crisis (Showalter and Jones, 1985). In other instances, inmates reach out to their wives or girlfriends and family members primarily in an attempt to make a favorable impression on the parole board, exaggerating the quality of these relationships (Rieger, 1973). This can be interpreted as "a deliberate misrepresentation based on their need for outside contacts" (Hannon et al., 1984, 258).

Effects on Wives

Although inmates suffer a loss of freedom and are separated from family, friends, and community, wives too are negatively affected by their husbands' incarceration. Most often they become an invisible minority with many unmet needs resulting from their husbands' incarceration. Most wives experience problems in a variety of areas and need concrete help in securing child care, financial assistance, affordable housing, and emotional support (Fishman, 1990; Morris, 1965; Schneller, 1975a).

Wives' views about the effects of their husbands' incarceration on their marriages vary according to several factors, such as the type of crime committed, marital functioning prior to the arrest and incarceration, length of sentence and time served in prison by their husbands, and their own beliefs about the criminal justice system (Morris, 1965). A minority of wives has been found to be relieved that their husbands have been imprisoned (Morris, 1965; Swan, 1981). Some wives have admitted that their lives improved as a result of their husbands' incarceration, citing alcoholism, jealous rage, substance abuse, and domestic violence as frequent occurrences prior to their imprisonments (Morris, 1965).

The studies already cited indicate that some wives are relatively untroubled by their husbands' incarceration. But more frequently, the research suggests that a psychological crisis occurs. Even before their husbands are imprisoned wives typically experience distress. First, the process of arrest and arraignment causes many wives to suffer from anxiety, worry, depression, and discouragement (Schwartz and Weintraub, 1974; Swan, 1981). These psychological stresses, in combination with preexisting marital difficulties, may cause some relationships to deteriorate. One study found that almost half of the marriages ended in separation or divorce prior to the actual incarceration (Swan, 1981).

Once a husband has entered prison, feelings of loneliness, sexual frustration, and fear and anxiety about his safety are frequently cited to be concerns of inmates' wives (Howlett, 1973; Schneller, 1975a; Swan, 1981). Insufficient information about their husbands' status and whereabouts within the prison also contributes to wives' emotional distress (Schwartz and Weintraub, 1974). In addition, most wives soon begin to be concerned about their husbands' adjustment once they are released (Morris, 1965).

The majority of wives also has financial problems as a result of their husbands' incarceration (Morris, 1965). Most were poor even before their husbands were imprisoned, many had received public assistance (Schneller, 1975a). Wives who are employed typically work as semi-skilled workers, usually in pink collar jobs (Morris, 1965). Some wives become distressed as a result of having to enter the labor force for the first time while managing a home and raising a family alone under very trying circumstances (Morris, 1965). Frequently, wives move as a result of perceived stigma, financial problems, or in the attempt to be closer their husbands' correctional facility (Fishman, 1990).

Like the wives of military personnel, spouses of prisoners have been found to withdraw from social contacts, becoming *de facto* single parents and expressing resentment about their husbands' lack of participation in child rearing duties (Morris, 1965; Rosenfeld et al., 1973). Even when extended family support is available, wives to a large extent must cope with their children alone (Bakker et al., 1978; Hinds, 1981; Swan, 1981). Most wives of inmates find being a single parent a lonely experience and have difficulty managing the children (Howlett, 1973; Morris, 1965). Thus, becoming a single parent while still being married and working full-time is a difficult task that affects the wife's psychosocial adjustment along with several other factors, including the quality of her coping prior to her husband's incarceration.

In addition, some investigators have found that those families receiving support from friends and family members cope more effectively than those who do not receive such support (Morris, 1965; Swan, 1981). Relatives and friends have been found to offer practical assistance such as providing child care, lending money, and providing emotional support (Swan, 1981). However, others have observed that while relatives offer some support, it is not sufficient (Schneller, 1975b; Schwartz and Weintraub, 1974).

Although inmates frequently believe that the extended family is helping, the research evidence is not conclusive on the extent or adequacy of this assistance (Schwartz and Weintraub, 1974). Often the inmate's parents blame the wife for his criminal behavior and may be critical of her management of the children and the household, leading them to withhold practical or emotional support (Schwartz and Weintraub, 1974). In addition, the wife's parents may also be less supportive and helpful than she would like. (Apparently this lack of practical support is a problem for female inmates as well [Kiser, 1991]). Her parents may also criticize her for having gotten involved with the offender. Once he is incarcerated this may evolve into open resentment of him and the marriage as a result of the strain placed on their daughter and grandchildren. This may lead the wife's parents to pressure her to divorce her husband. If she fails to acquiesce to their wishes, they may be less than enthusiastic in the emotional and concrete support they supply to their daughter (Schwartz and Weintraub, 1974). A common-law wife may fare less well than a legally married wife in terms of assistance from her own family and the inmate's parents, due to the more ambiguous status of her relationship with the inmate (Schneller, 1975a).

One universal problem encountered by wives is what and how to tell the children about their fathers' absence. Although some parents tell children the truth, others avoid the subject altogether, and still others fabricate explanations, such as that he or she is away at school or in the hospital (Crosthwaite, 1972; Fishman, 1981; Kiser, 1991; Sack, 1977). The reasons underlying this misinformation are first, the shame and guilt associated with the husband's criminal behavior, arrest, and subsequent imprisonment and second, the belief that young children in particular cannot understand what being in prison means (Hinds, 1981). Female inmates are also said to deceive their children regarding their true whereabouts, especially young children (Kiser, 1991).

To summarize, being an inmate is difficult, but being the wife of a prisoner may be equally difficult. Wives often feel that they too are "doing time." Both inmates and their wives must learn to cope with psychological stress emanating from separation from one another, punitive societal attitudes, uncertainty, disruption of their lives, and disappointment about the future. Support from a social network and assistance from human services have been found to enhance the wife's ability to cope with the stress of a husband's incarceration.

Effects on Children

A father's absence from a child's life for any reason can cause disruptions in psychological and social development (Rosenfeld et al., 1973; Public/Private Ventures, 1990). Although children of inmates have not been studied extensively or systematically, a father's imprisonment has been linked to social, emotional, and cognitive delays in children (Friedman and Esselstyn, 1965). Limited research suggests that they have behavioral problems at home and at school and suffer from emotional distress, worry, and depression as a result of the loss of their father and other associated difficulties (Sack, 1971; Swan, 1981).

Children's needs for their imprisoned fathers are especially pronounced when they have had a positive relationship with him prior to his incarceration (Sack, 1977). Visitation opportunities can help to maintain the relationship where it has been strong and can contribute to development of a more positive relationship where it needs strengthening (Sack, 1977). However, sometimes the incarcerated father has difficulty in knowing how to relate to a child with whom he does not live or spend much time. This may lead him to spoil the child, creating problems for the caretaking parent left at home (Hughes, 1982; Rosenfeld et al., 1973). Ultimately, visits to prison, while helpful to both child and parent, are a poor substitute for an ongoing relationship.

During the arrest, trial, and early imprisonment period children acutely mourn the loss of their father. They have been found to exhibit an array of emotional reactions including denial, guilt, anger, and sadness about his incarceration (Fishman, 1981; Fishman, 1990; Sack, 1977; Swan, 1981; Thompson, 1984). The depth of a child's mourning reaction, however, depends on the quality of relationship, the type of crime committed, and the accuracy of the information provided to the child about what happened to the father. For example, children who have been told that their father

is a sex offender or who have been victims of incest may not miss
their father a great deal (Morris, 1967).

In many cases, parents do not provide full information to their
children about their father's whereabouts (Morris, 1965; Sack,
1977). This may be the case even when the child has witnessed the
arrest (Thompson, 1984). Mothers and fathers regularly use deception or distortion of the facts in an attempt to deny to themselves
the painful truth about where the father is and why (Fishman, 1981;
1983; Fishman, 1990; Showalter and Jones, 1980; Thompson,
1984). The parents' reluctance to acknowledge a father's incarceration may also serve as a means of shielding themselves from
worries and anxieties about his safety (Wilmer et al., 1966). But a
child who is not told the truth experiences confusion, worry,
feelings of rejection, blockage of normal grieving processes, and
disturbances in behavior, and they may discover through other
means where their father actually is (Morris, 1965; Sack, 1977;
Showalter and Jones, 1980; Swan, 1981). Thus, failure to communicate the truth to the child can contribute to additional anger and
serious behavioral and emotional problems (Showalter and Jones,
1980).

Wives of prisoners often report that their children become more
of a problem during incarceration than prior to it (Sack et al., 1976).
There may be an increase in antisocial behavior and aggressiveness
during the prison term (Crosthwaite, 1972; Fishman, 1981; 1983;
Fishman, 1990; Fritsch and Burkhead, 1981; Sack et al., 1976;
Sack, 1977; Thompson, 1984). Boys and girls may also become
truant from school and disobedient at home (Crosthwaite, 1972;
Gaudin, 1984; Sack et al., 1976). Some studies suggest that the
sudden increase in belligerent behavior occurs within two months
of the father's incarceration (Sack, 1977). Other findings indicate
that disobedient behavior is exacerbated for pubescent or early
adolescent boys (Sack et al., 1976). Girls may fare even worse than
boys by becoming sexually precocious or pregnant (Crosthwaite,
1972). It is also not uncommon for children to blame their mothers
for the incarceration or the problems associated with it (Fishman,
1990; Lowenstein, 1986; Sack, 1977).

Some factors associated with the extent of children's acting-out behavior are the quality of the relationship with their imprisoned father, the quality of the mother-child relationship, overidentification with their father's criminal behavior, and feeling guilty or responsible for his incarceration (Sack, 1977; Schwartz and Weintraub, 1974).

Frequently, a father's imprisonment results in the family's loss of income, which in turn leads to frequent moves and changes in schools for the children. This additional disruption in a child's life on top of having a father in prison can result in teasing and taunting by peers (Sack, 1976). Not being able to make close friendships and having poor parent-child relationships may lead to low self-esteem and poor self-concept (Moerck, 1973; Sack et al., 1977). Somatic problems have also been noted among the children of inmates, such as enuresis, nightmares, or insomnia, as has loss of appetite (Fishman, 1990).

Children's problems may extend into the reentry period of their father's release from incarceration. Parents may become preoccupied with one another and the strain of reorganizing the family, and may overlook their child's need for attention and involvement with them. Children, too, may have unrealistic expectations about their father's return to the home, and neither the parents nor the children may receive adequate preparation for the reentry of the father into their daily lives (Fishman, 1981; 1983; Fishman, 1990; Thompson, 1984).

To conclude, a number of factors can moderate the impact of a father's incarceration on a child's psychological and emotional adjustment. The degree of support from extended family members, a good mother-child relationship, and community responsiveness to children's special needs enhance the likelihood of a child's adjustment. The impact of the father's imprisonment on the mother, as well as the quality of father-child relationship prior to incarceration, are also factors (Morris, 1967).

In summary, incarceration of a father can have a variety of effects on children. Often parents fail to be honest with children about the father's whereabouts, potentially exacerbating the child's reactions. Responses include general emotional distress, a profound grief reaction, behavioral problems such as disobedience and aggressiveness, alienation from peers, and somatic complaints, such as sleeping difficulties. These responses are mediated by a number of variables. The nature of the offense, the length of prison sentence, the time remaining in prison, the degree of stigma associated with the criminal behavior, the extent of father's involvement with the child prior to incarceration, the family's closeness, the quality of the marital relationship prior to incarceration, and the family's coping resources have all been identified as intervening factors in children's adjustment to incarceration (Hairston, 1988; Lowenstein, 1986).

FAMILY RESPONSE TO INCARCERATION

Our earlier discussion of stress, crisis, and coping introduced a general model of family response to stressful events. Here, the discussion turns to specific ways in which inmates and wives cope with the experience of incarceration. Particular attention is paid to family visits and home furloughs as possible coping strategies.

Wife Coping

In applying these theoretical premises to families of inmates, certain specific behaviors have been found to enhance coping and adaptation. The wife's ability to become economically self-sufficient and maintain a job is a primary task that must be addressed first. Difficulties may arise when the wife has few job skills, is underemployed, becomes burdened with emotional distress from the loss of her husband, or is caring for very young children or significant others. The development of relationships outside the immediate family and the strengthening of bonds to the community through procurement of social services have also been identified as facilitating wives' successful coping with temporary separation from their husbands (McCubbin, 1979). As discussed earlier, assistance in the areas of child care, emotional support, and transportation to and from correctional facilities can ease the burden of becoming an unanticipated and temporary single parent.

Other factors that enhance the wife's adaptation include involvement with organized religion, forming mutual support groups with other wives of inmates, being married to an inmate with a shorter sentence or to a first-time offender, being married to an inmate who did not play a contributing role in the family before incarceration, having more formal education, having older rather than younger children, and being skilled at setting limits with children (Burr, 1973; Fox, 1981; Lowenstein, 1984). Using a variety of active coping strategies results in the more successful psychological management of the wife's anxiety and depression and enhanced family stability and contributes to feelings of mastery during the initial and later stages of the imprisonment process (McCubbin, 1979; Morris, 1965).

A number of research studies have found that family support improves the wife's sense of emotional well-being and aids in the family's ability to recover from the loss of a father and husband. However, wives report that there is a discrepancy between the amount of assistance offered by their own families and their husbands' families (Schwartz and Weintraub, 1974). Assistance with child care, loans of money, and other concrete aid have been reported as being readily available from the wife's family, in contrast to the husband's family (Daniel and Barrett, 1981; Swan, 1981). "Were it not for help from their own families most wives would be seriously deprived both financially and emotionally" (Morris, 1965, 282). Furthermore, some wives report that their husbands' families become disengaged from them and the children (Daniel and Barrett, 1981; Morris, 1965; Swan, 1981). Whereas the inmate's family often blames the wife for their son's arrest, her family may place contingencies on their help, suggesting, for example, that she divorce him (Swan, 1981). Obviously, estrangement from either the inmate's family or her own can contribute to problems within the marriage and for the children.

Inmate Coping

The maintenance of contact between the inmate and his spouse, children, extended family members, and friends assists him in adjusting to the prison environment. A close relationship between the inmate and his family results in less tension, better feelings about himself, and improved prison behavior, predicting higher parole success (Cavan and Zemans, 1958; Kaslow, 1978). More frequent contact helps family solidarity and feelings of closeness. Furthermore, the ability of the inmate, spouse, and family to acknowledge to one another that they can be mutually supportive and can successfully adapt to trying times may reduce the inmate's worry about his family (Fishman and Alissi, 1979).

Letter writing, phone calls, and prison visits have been the traditional means used to maintain relationships between inmates and their loved ones (Kaslow, 1978). These forms of communication, however, have serious limitations as means of maintaining family ties.

Prison Visits. Visiting a loved one in prison can be very frustrating, anxiety producing, and ultimately unsatisfactory for both the visitors and the inmate. First, correctional facilities are usually located a long distance from the inmate's home, insofar as most are sited in rural areas while the majority of inmates are from urban areas. Commutes to the prison can, therefore, be difficult for visitors because of inadequate public transportation and/or the lack of access to an automobile, as well as the transportation's cost (Freedman and Rice, 1977; Weintraub, 1976). Reliance on extended family, neighbors, friends, and human service agencies for transportation to the prison may provide some limited assistance (Weintraub, 1976). Visits to the prison may also be frustrating because they are brief, infrequent, and lack privacy (Freedman and Rice, 1977).

Designed to address concerns about the introduction of contraband such as drugs and weapons, procedures and policies governing visits can be complex and difficult to comprehend. Two national surveys of correctional settings regarding their policies governing visiting by inmates' children found broad variability across facilities and substantial restrictions regarding such visitation. For example, although all states had policies regulating contact between inmates and family members, few states permitted physical contact between inmates and children, which would be very difficult for children to understand or comply with (Bennett, 1989; Hairston and Hess, 1989).

Most facilities restrict children's freedom of movement during visits and do not provide special facilities for those with young children, such as changing areas, play areas, or refrigeration for formula, despite the number of very young children who are likely to be visiting with their parents (Bauhofer, 1987). In most facilities the inmate and his adult visitors are expected to control their children, who may be irritable and rambunctious after a lengthy, tiring trip to the prison. Under these circumstances children can become demanding in their need for attention at a time when the parent may also be tired and stressed but is in need of reconnecting with the inmate. Thus, having a special area in the visiting room where children can play, supervised by trained adults, is important for making the visits as pleasurable as possible for everyone concerned. And yet, Hairston and Hess (1989) found that only Missouri, New York, and South Carolina routinely provided activity centers for children to use while visiting. Prison overcrowding is not likely to improve this situation.

Other Forms of Communication. Telephoning home is another means of maintaining contact with loved ones; however, it is expensive. Also, the length of calls may be regulated and in some cases monitored by prison security (Fishman, 1990; Freedman and Rice, 1977). Many inmates write to their family members at home, but letter writing may inhibit self-disclosure. Letters, too, may be imbued with magical thinking about family life on release. Additionally, letter writing may not be a very effective means of communication, especially if the inmate has poor writing skills. The shame and embarrassment associated with illiteracy may also inhibit the writing of letters (Freedman and Rice, 1977).

Conjugal Visits and Furloughs

In some states, correctional policy has become more enlightened and progressive regarding the importance of visiting. A few states permit the family members of certain inmates to have overnight visits at the prison facility (so-called conjugal visits) and/or permit some inmates to be furloughed home. One objective of furloughs and the major purpose of conjugal visits is to strengthen family ties, thereby aiding in postrelease adjustment (Haynor, 1972; Hopper, 1967; Howser et al., 1983). In the United States both programs have been controversial and closely scrutinized due to the public's concern and beliefs about community safety, the view of incarceration as punishment for a crime, and moral judgments concerning sexuality.

Internationally, however, many countries allow for some sort of personal contact between the inmate and the family (Cavan and Zemans, 1958; Balogh, 1964). In contrast to the common American philosophy of viewing inmate contact with family members as a privilege rather than a right, many other countries do not view the deprivation of "marital privileges" as a vital element of the punishment process (Balogh, 1964). In Latin American countries and other Third World countries such as India and the Philippines, for example, conjugal visits are viewed as helping to promote family solidarity and prisoner well-being, thereby aiding in the management of the prison facility (Balogh, 1964).

Conjugal Visits. Currently, seven states have conjugal visit programs in the United States (Goetting, 1982). California, Connecticut, Minnesota, Mississippi, New York, South Carolina, and Washington are reported to have on-site, overnight family visitation programs (Goetting, 1982; Hopper, 1967). Mississippi and South Carolina have the oldest institutionalized programs allowing for personal and intimate contact between inmates and significant others (Goetting, 1982).

The states that permit overnight stays at the prison facilities primarily allow for parents, spouses, children, and other designated family members to visit the inmate. Visits occur in specifically designed areas, usually trailers, last from seven to seventy-two hours, and occur at two to three month intervals. The common requirements of most states include (1) having served some portion of one's sentence, (2) maintaining a good prison disciplinary record, and (3) not being eligible for parole at the time of the visit (Goetting, 1982).

To be eligible for extended visits with one's spouse in New York State, an inmate must be legally married, have a relatively long sentence, and not be eligible for parole. The objective of the program is to strengthen family ties and facilitate postrelease adjustment (Howser et al., 1983). Although the Federal Bureau of Prisons has recommended that inmates and their wives receive concomitant family counseling prior to and following overnight visits, this is not a requirement in New York State (Goetting, 1982).

There is very little research examining the impact of conjugal visits. In a study comparing inmates who had conjugal visits with those who did not, Burstein (1977) found that there were transportation problems for wives and family members and feelings of anxiety and depression after the visits for the inmates. But wives felt that they were able to share their everyday lives and difficulties, problem solve together, discuss financial concerns, and communicate about the children (Burstein, 1977). Research conducted by the New York State Department of Corrections on 1,129 inmates who had participated in its Family Reunion Program (FRP) yielded two valuable findings: Participants have improved discipline records while incarcerated and are less likely to be returned to custody compared with nonparticipants (Howser et al., 1983; Howser and MacDonald, 1982). The authors concluded that the program does strengthen family ties and promote community integration on release.

A 1981 research study comparing the views of prison administrators about furlough programs versus conjugal visits concluded that only a small portion of inmates can participate in conjugal visits due to limitations on physical space and eligibility requirements. In addition, since many facilities are old and costs for expanding facilities or adding trailers are prohibitively high during times of prison overcrowding and compete with the financial needs of other programs, a serious barrier to expansion of conjugal visit programs was noted. Objections were also raised on the basis of administrative problems involving contraband and security. There were additional questions regarding whether or not to include common-law marriages and girlfriends, as well as staff ambivalence about the overall value of the conjugal visit programs. Finally, prison administrators were sensitive to community expectations about inmates serving "hard time" for their crimes and community values about sexuality, both of which might be threatened by broader implementation of family visiting programs (Balogh, 1964; Goetting, 1982; Johns, 1971). Thus, the federal prison system and most states do not currently permit extended (overnight) family visits to correctional facilities.

Furlough Programs. Because of these concerns, furlough programs have been suggested as an alternative to conjugal visit programs. Many federal and state policy administrators preferred furloughs to conjugal visits as a means for inmates to maintain family ties, based on the rationale that furlough programs are easier to administer and permit more widespread inmate participation (Goetting, 1982).

Furloughs are temporary leaves from prison lasting from four hours to thirty days, the modal length being forty-eight to seventy-two hours. Furloughs are granted for a variety of reasons, the most common of which are: funerals; medical reasons or emergencies; visits with family; seeking employment; religious reasons; and promoting community reintegration. Not every state grants furloughs for all of these reasons, and only a small subset permits furloughs to visit one's family. In addition, virtually all states have eligibility requirements that greatly limit which inmates may qualify for these temporary leaves. The most common eligibility requirements are that the inmate (1) has served a minimum amount of his sentence; (2) is near his release date or eligible for parole; (3) has a good institutional adjustment record; and (4) has not committed certain heinous crimes, such as violent crimes or sex offenses. In addition, many states limit eligibility to minimum security inmates or those in community custody (Marlette, 1990).

Correctional administrators have been found to believe that furlough programs are more flexible than conjugal visits and are more cost effective, freeing money to be spent on other needed programs that benefit more inmates. In addition, home visits are thought to be more natural than conjugal visits, which can be very artificial because they take place in a trailer at the correctional facility. Furloughs are also seen as a more effective means of helping families and correctional personnel in prerelease planning (Johns, 1971; Markley, 1973). Like conjugal visits, participation in home furloughs has been found to be associated with lower recidivism, as compared with rates predicted by the Base Expectancy Table (LeClair, 1978).

However, data on furlough programs suggest that furloughs may not be the viable alternative to conjugal visits that many prison administrators have suggested. A 1988 survey of the fifty states, the District of Columbia, and the Federal Bureau of Prisons indicated that all states but two (New Hampshire and Nevada), as well as the District of Columbia and the federal prison system, have furlough programs. However, very few inmates were able to participate in those programs due to the restrictive eligibility requirements (Marlette, 1990).

As a result, only 55,000 inmates actually received furloughs in 1988. However, that figure was obtained just before the 1988 presidential campaign in which the notorious Willie Horton incident occurred. Horton was a Massachusetts inmate out on furlough who brutally attacked a Maryland couple, raping the wife and stabbing the husband. Despite successful completion rates nationally (almost half of the systems granting furloughs had success rates in excess of 98% in 1987), this incident has had a chilling effect on furlough programs across the country. Thus, it is anticipated that even fewer home furloughs will be granted in the future (Marlette, 1990).

In conclusion, furloughs for a variety of purposes are an effective means of permitting a relatively small number of inmates to spend time in the community. However, they are not the panacea suggested by prison officials in Goetting's (1982) study. Nor are they a viable alternative to conjugal visit programs in meeting the objective of maintaining meaningful ties between inmates and their families. Many inmates do not qualify for furloughs, and even those who do may not be able to take advantage of such a leave until the end of their sentence. By then, family ties for many have become irreparably broken.

But despite the limitations, the evidence suggests that both furloughs and conjugal visits can assist in maintaining family ties (Burstein, 1977; Fox, 1981; Howser and MacDonald, 1982). Although there is a high divorce rate for inmates, the rate of recidivism is lower for those who maintain strong family relationships (Burstein, 1977). Research suggests that visits from family members are even more important than postrelease employment in reducing the likelihood of returning to prison (Fox, 1981; Holt and Miller, 1972). Thus, the family can play a major role in the inmate's rehabilitation, but their influence is directly proportional to how well the family copes with the incarceration (Fox, 1981).

In one early study, for example, parolees who had had weekly contact with their families while in prison and received marital/family support were more successful after release from prison than were those who lacked regular family contact and support (Glaser, 1964). However, over time, broken family ties increase the likelihood of committing a new crime and being returned to prison (Pueschel and Moglia, 1977). According to Holt and Miller's (1972) classic California study, there is a "strong and consistent positive relationship that exists between parole success and maintaining strong family ties while in prison" (v). Holt and Miller (1972) further suggested that:

> the positive relationship between strength of social ties and success in parole has held up for 45 years of release across very diverse offender populations and in different localities. It is doubtful if there is any other research finding in the field of corrections which can approximate this record (Holt and Miller, 1972, 61).

Strong family ties were found to be independent of other factors associated with successful parole such as a job or a place to live (Holt and Miller, 1972).

Summary

A number of variables predict wives' successful coping with the incarceration of their husbands. These include involvement in roles outside the home; economic self-sufficiency; a strong social support network, especially contact with and practical and emotional support from their own and their husbands' extended families; and use of active coping strategies to manage their responses to their spouses' imprisonment.

As measured by positive institutional adjustment and lack of recidivism, married inmates cope most effectively when they maintain family ties with their wives and children. Ties are maintained through the traditional means of communication, namely letters, telephone calls, visits, and home furloughs. In addition, a small number of states permit extended (overnight) visits with family members, which are called conjugal visits when wives stay with their husbands. Although family contact has been associated with both good institutional adjustment and decreased recidivism, the current correctional policy and funding climate does not look optimistic for expanding conjugal visit programs.

Chapter 3

Research Methods

This study was undertaken with several broad objectives in mind. The first was to better understand the impact of incarceration on inmate families. The second goal was to identify methods of coping commonly used by married inmates and their wives to deal with the stresses associated with imprisonment of a husband and father. Another goal was to learn more about the salience of the father role to this inmate population. The final objective was to learn more about the effects of a conjugal visit program on inmate couples.

At the outset we had hoped to use the literature reviewed in Chapter 2 to formulate hypotheses about coping and the impact of the Family Reunion Program (FRP) that could be empirically tested using our sample of inmates and wives. However, the limitations of that literature has prevented us from generating specific hypotheses, and instead a series of questions were formulated that are explored in the data. In the end formal hypotheses are generated that can be used to guide future research on the effects of incarceration on family life.

RESEARCH QUESTIONS

Coping

A major goal of the study was to explore coping strategies used by inmates and their wives and to determine if coping was enhanced among those who were permitted regular conjugal visits. The following questions were posed:

1. How well do inmates and their wives cope with the experience of incarceration?
2. What kinds of supports are received by wives and how adequate are they to meet their needs?
3. How extensive is communication between inmates and their wives, and what forms does it take?
4. What factors are associated with enhanced coping on the part of inmates and wives?

Quality of Marital Relationships

As discussed in Chapter 2, incarceration tends to have a deleterious effect on most marital relationships. Thus, we were interested in better understanding the quality of the marital relationships achieved by couples in the study and how well they functioned as marital units. Accordingly we asked:

5. How cohesive, adaptable, and satisfied with their relationships are these couples? How close do they feel to one another? How is decision making distributed between the spouses, and has that changed over time?

The Family Reunion Program

A major thrust of the research was an in depth study of the conjugal visit program sponsored by the New York State Department of Correctional Services (NYSDOCS), called the Family Reunion Program or FRP. Whereas certain aspects of the program have been studied, many questions about its impact on the participating couples remain unanswered. The questions we posed are:

6. How often do Family Reunion visits take place and what occurs during a typical visit?
7. What is the perceived impact of FRP visits on inmates, wives, and children?
8. Is participation in FRP associated with enhanced coping?
9. Are there differences in inmate-wife communication based on FRP participation?
10. Are there differences in decision making based on FRP participation?
11. Are couples who have participated in FRP more cohesive, more adaptable, and more satisfied with their marriages than those who have not participated?
12. Are inmates and their wives who have participated in FRP closer to one another than those who have not participated?
13. Are inmates who have participated in FRP closer to their children than those who have not participated?

DESIGN

The NYSDOCS initiated a program in 1976 that permits inmates with "good institutional adjustment" and no major disciplinary problems to have extended (overnight) family visits for forty-eight hours (Howser et al., 1983). At the time of the study the program was available at thirteen out of the fifty or more correctional facilities in the state. Visits take place in private, three-bedroom mobile homes in secure locations on the facility grounds. Utilities, kitchen utensils, a television, and bedding are provided, as well as playground equipment for children. Visitors must secure their own transportation and provide food for the visit. Contraband, including alcohol, illegal drugs, and weapons are prohibited, and family members are not permitted to leave the site during the visits except for emergencies.

The objective of FRP is to solidify and support family ties, thereby facilitating postrelease adjustment. An inmate must be legally married to have his wife participate in the overnight visits.

Thus, common-law wives may not participate. Other family members may also participate, for example, parents, brothers, sisters, uncles, and so forth. However, since we were interested in whether or not conjugal visits between spouses are associated with better family functioning we chose not to study the effects of inmate visits with other family members.

A formative, descriptive study was undertaken involving inmates and their wives who had participated in FRP, who were legally married for at least two years, and who had children together. Participating inmates came from five facilities, three maximum security (one with FRP and two without FRP) and two medium security (one with FRP and one without).

Procedures

After visiting the five facilities to negotiate permission to perform the study, cooperation was obtained from Family Service or Volunteer Coordinators. These staff members assisted in recruitment of the sample by approaching potential participants and informing them about the study. This was accomplished via a handout prepared by the authors and approved by the Department of Correctional Services. Any inmate who had had multiple Family Reunion visits with his wife and had at least one child was eligible. For nonFRP sites, coordinators were asked to screen inmates and approach those who would qualify for FRP if such a program existed at that facility. Since FRP eligibility is available only to inmates with good institutional adjustment and absence of serious disciplinary problems, only inmates with this profile were approached by correctional staff to participate in the contrast group. In addition, only married inmates with children were recruited in the attempt to match the contrast group to the FRP group. The authors and trained graduate students in social work interviewed the participants for approximately one hour.

The Sample

Inmates. The sample consisted of sixty-three inmates and thirty-nine of their wives. In all, thirty-three inmates were currently in the FRP and thirty were not; twenty-seven wives were in the FRP group and twelve were not. Half of the inmate sample came from maximum security facilities ($n = 31$), and half were drawn from medium security facilities ($n = 30$).

Comparability of the FRP group and the contrast group. The inmates studied can be considered among the best adjusted of the inmate population because of the selection criteria for FRP and the matching criteria for the contrast group. The fact of being married itself is rather atypical in a population where most inmates are not currently married. FRP inmates had been married an average of 16.24 years in contrast to nonFRP inmates who were married for a mean of 9.67 years, a statistically nonsignificant difference. FRP inmates had an average of 2.61 children, compared to 1.96 children in the nonFRP group, again not a signficant difference. Regarding the ethnic distribution of our sample, it is overwhelmingly non-white (21% white, 37% black and 37% Hispanic), which very closely approximates the New York State prison population, as well as that of other large states such as California, Texas, and Florida. Mean age overall was 37.35, with a range of twenty-five to sixty-one years. This is somewhat older, on average, than New York State male inmates in general, about half of whom are under age thirty and one-third of whom are between age thirty and forty. The FRP inmates were significantly older than nonFRP inmates, $\overline{X} = 40.12$ compared to 31.64 ($t = 3.30$, $df = 41$, $p < .002$). FRP inmates had been incarcerated for 4.36 years on average and would not be eligible for parole for another 6.29 years on average. NonFRP inmates had been imprisoned for a mean of 3.33 years and would be eligible for parole in 7.25 years on average. Neither of these differences was statistically significant. There is a nonsignificant trend for FRP inmates to be more likely not to have previous arrests and less likely to have two or more previous arrests compared to nonFRP inmates. Half or fewer of both samples had been incarcerated previously. Thus, the two groups were determined to be comparable on most of the important dimensions with the exception of age.

To determine if age differences might affect the results, Pearson product-moment correlations were computed separately for each group for age and other important variables. Results indicated that age was significantly associated only with number of children [$r(29) = .39, p < .04$ for FRP and $r(11) = .66, p < .03$ for non-FRP], number of previous arrests for nonFRP only [$r(13) = .70, p < .008$], and length of marriage for FRP only [$r(21) = .78, p < .0001$]. It is not surprising that being older would be associated with being married longer and having more children, as well as having a longer arrest record. This was not seen as being problematic in terms of analyses of the variables of interest.

Sample in relation to inmates nationally. There are some noteworthy differences between the sample we studied and incarcerated men nationally. All participating inmates were married, whereas only about 20% of male inmates overall are married. In addition, this sample was more likely to be nonwhite, which is characteristic of New York State's inmate population. Nationally, only 12% of all inmates are Hispanic, in contrast to 37% of our sample; likewise, whereas 47% of inmates overall are black, only 37% of our inmate sample was black (Jamieson and Flanagan, 1989). Thus, although one must be cautious in generalizing our findings to other inmate populations, our ability to generalize to married inmates in New York State and other similar states is good.

Wives. All wives were invited to be interviewed. Two refused to participate, and six indicated they they were separated from the inmate by the time they were contacted. Refusals and separations were evenly divided between the FRP and nonFRP groups. Fourteen wives were interviewed in person at the facility in conjunction with a regular visit; twenty-five others preferred a phone interview. The remainder (thirteen) could not be located despite persistent efforts to find them. This may have resulted because their spouses were confined in facilities designated as temporary. These men were transferred rather quickly and could not be located to obtain information regarding their wives' whereabouts. In addition, two inmates had been released and could not be found by the time we began to approach the wives. Of the wives who could not be located, three did not have phones and could not be found despite attempts to contact them through a neighbor or family member. Those who could not be located were more likely to be from the nonFRP group, resulting in the smaller sample size for that group. This was determined to be an artifact of the particular facility where their husbands were confined, which was seen by the Department of Corrections as a transitional placement. The difficulty experienced in locating and interviewing these prison wives closely parallels that of Morris (1965) in her study of British wives of inmates.

Wives tended to be the same ethnicity as their husbands. They had an average of 2.43 children. Most were employed (60%), generally at pink-collar jobs. Most of the remainder received Public Assistance. Ninety-five percent of the wives lived in their own apartments or homes, although the majority expressed dissatisfaction with their current living situations for a variety of reasons, most often because their husbands were not with them.

Measures

A structured interview schedule was developed based on the incarceration and family life literature. Inmates were asked closed- and open-ended questions regarding prison life. The design of the instrument was influenced by the ABCX model of family stress and coping. We endeavored to include as many aspects of the model as possible that affect how families adapt to and recover from crisis or stressful situations.

The areas covered in the inmate questionnaire included: the means of communication (telephone calls, letters, and visits) with his wife and children and their perceived impact on family relationships; the quality of relationship with and perceived closeness to wife and children; relevant childhood experiences; perceptions of the father role; family decision making currently and prior to incarceration; sources of stress and means of coping with stress; and for FRP participants, what occurred during trailer visits and how they felt about the visits.

Inmate-family communication was measured by asking the following questions:

1. "How often do you see your wife?" Response categories were "about once a week or more, about every two weeks, about once a month, about every two to three months, about every six months."

2. "Do you talk [write letters] to your wife on the telephone?" Those answering "yes" were asked "How often?" with the following response categories: "more than once a week, once a week, once every two weeks, once a month, less than once a month," and were asked, "What kinds of things do you talk [write] about?"

3. "What kind of effect do these calls have on your relationship with your wife, do they make it better, have no effect, or make it worse?"

4. "How often do you see your children?" with the following response categories: "weekly, every two weeks, once a month, every two to three months, every six months." Those who responded using any category other than "weekly" were then asked "Why don't you see them more often?"

5. "Do you talk [write letters] to your children on the telephone?" Those answering yes were asked "How often?" using the same response categories as in (2) above. Those indicating that they wrote letters were asked "What kinds of things do you write about?"

6. "What kind of effect do these calls have on your relationship with your children, do they make it better, have no effect, or make it worse?"

Perceived closeness to spouses and children was measured by asking "How close do [did] you feel to your wife [children, husband] at the present time [before FRP]?" Responses were recorded on a seven-point scale anchored at one (very distant) and seven (very close).

A series of questions was posed regarding how decision making is distributed between husbands and wives, both currently and prior to the husbands' incarceration. Response categories were coded as (1) "husband always," (2) "husband most of the time," (3) "husband and wife equally," (4) "wife most of the time," and (5) "wife always." Categories 1 and 2 were combined, as were 4 and 5, to simplify presentation of the findings in Chapter 5.

The general question asked was "How are decisions made in the following matters," then reading the response categories listed above. The specific areas included:

1. "When children should be disciplined";
2. "When the children are old enough to try new things, for example, going somewhere alone";
3. "When to make major purchases, for instance, new furniture";
4. "How much to spend on food, clothes, allowance, etc.";
5. "Where the family should live"; and
6. "Related to [your spouse's] job outside the home."

Regarding those in the FRP, inmates were asked how long they had participated in the program (in months) and how many visits their wife had made. In addition they were asked:

1. "What kinds of things do you do on the visits?"
2. "Do you spend time alone with your wife [any of the children]?"
3. "How do you feel about these visits?"
4. "How do your children feel about these visits?"
5. "Has your relationship with your wife [children] changed as a result of the trailer visits?" Those answering "yes" were asked "In what ways?"

Sources of stress were measured by asking "What have you found to be the most stressful things about prison life?" Means of coping with stress were measured in two ways, first by asking "What kinds of things do you do to help deal with those stresses?" In addition, at the end of the interview inmates responded to the Family Crisis Oriented Personal Evaluations Scales (F-COPES), a coping inventory described later.

Wives were asked similar questions (except for feelings about prison life) but were also asked about living circumstances, sources of practical and emotional support, and children's problems. Sources of stress ("What has been the most stressful part of your husband's being in prison?") and coping mechanisms ("What kinds of things have you found to be most helpful in dealing with the stresses you described above, related to your husband's being away?") were tapped. Wives also responded to the F-COPES at the end of the interview.

Sources of practical and social support from extended family and neighbors were measured by asking,

1. "How frequently do you see members of your own family, such as your mother, father, sister, brother, stepparents, etc.?" Possible response categories were "every day, about two to three times a week, about once a week, about once every two weeks, about once a month, less than once a month."

2. "Do they provide you with assistance of any kind, for example, lending money, providing food, babysitting, etc.?" This was followed with "What kinds of things do they do?" for those who responded "yes."

3. "Do members of your family provide emotional support to you while your husband is in prison?" Those responding "yes" were then asked, "How have they been supportive?"

4. "Are there things your family is not doing that you wish they were doing to help or support you since your husband has been in prison?" This was followed with "What kinds of things would you like them to do?" for those who answered "yes."

5. "How frequently do you see members of your husband's family, such as his mother, father, sister, brother, etc.?" The same response categories listed in (1) were employed.

6. "Do they provide you with assistance of any kind, for example, lending money, providing food, babysitting, etc.?" Those who answered "yes" were then asked, "What kinds of things do they do?"

7. "Do members of your husband's family provide emotional support to you while you husband is in prison?" This was followed with "How have they been supportive?" for those answering in the affirmative.

8. "Are there things your husband's family is not doing that you wish they were doing to help or support you since your husband has been in prison?" This was followed by "What kinds of things would you like them to do?" for those who answered "yes."

9. "Are you close to any of your neighbors?" Those answering "yes" were then asked, "How frequently do you see them?" using the same response categories listed in (1).

10. "Do they provide you with assistance of any kind, for example, lending money, providing food, babysitting, etc.?" Those answering "yes" were then asked, "What kinds of things do they do?"

Wives were asked parallel questions to the inmates regarding communication on the telephone and through letters. In addition, they were asked "How frequently do [the children] get to see their father?", with the following response categories: "about once a month or more, every one to three months, once every four to six months, about once a year." Wives were also asked parallel questions with regard to their participation in and feelings about the FRP.

At the end of the interviews participants were asked to complete two standardized, paper-and-pencil inventories, the Family Adaptability and Cohesion Evaluation Scales (FACES III) (Olson et al., 1985) and the F-COPES (McCubbin et al., 1981).

The F-COPES is a twenty-nine-item instrument based on Hill's (1965) ABCX crisis model. It was designed to assess a family's crisis-meeting resources and the perceived meaning of a potential crisis, that is, coping, broadly defined. Thus, it attempts to assess the "B" (family resources, strengths) and "C" (definition or appraisal of the stressful event) dimensions of Hill's model. It has been administered to several large samples of family members and refined. In addition, it has been shown to have good reliability and validity (McCubbin et al., 1981).

The F-COPES yields a total coping score as well as five subscales: (1) Acquiring Social Support, nine items measuring the family's ability to actively engage in obtaining support from extended family, friends, and so forth; (2) Reframing, eight items assessing the ability to "redefine stressful events in order to make them more manageable"; (3) Seeking Spiritual Support, four items measuring the family's ability to acquire support from organized religion; (4) Mobilizing the Family to Acquire and Accept Help, four items assessing the ability to seek community resources and accept help from those outside the family; and (5) Passive Appraisal, four items measuring the family's ability to accept problematic situations (such as incarceration) with a minimum of reactivity (McCubbin et al., 1981).

FACES III is a twenty-item, self-report measure developed by David Olson and his colleagues at the University of Minnesota (Olson et al., 1985). It measures family members' perceptions of family cohesion and adaptability. It has been administered to several thousand families, both nonproblem and dysfunctional, and has been found to have high reliability and validity. It is widely used in empirical research to distinguish between problem and nonproblem families and is commonly used by clinicians as well. This instrument can be used as one way of tapping the "T" (family pathology) factor in McCubbin and McCubbin's (1987) revised version of Hill's family crisis model.

A major strength of the FACES III is that it yields norms and cutting points that allow placement of individual families or groups of families in their two-dimensional scheme, called the "circumplex model," simultaneously examining cohesion and adaptability in relation to one another. Cohesion scores place families in one of four ranges (disengaged, separated, connected, or enmeshed) based on their degree of emotional bonding to one another. Optimal functioning occurs in the separated and connected ranges. Adaptability scores identify families as rigid, structured, flexible, or chaotic depending on their ability to alter the family power structure, roles, and rules in response to situational or developmental stress. Structured and flexible families are considered most adaptive (Olson et al., 1985).

Family satisfaction is measured by having family members respond twice to the FACES, first for how they perceive the family to actually function, and again for how they would ideally like it to be. Family satisfaction is operationalized as the sum of the differences between how the family is perceived to function currently in contrast to how the person wishes it would function. It is the inverse of the total discrepancy between actual and ideal cohesion and adaptability that constitutes each individual's family satisfaction score; that is, smaller values indicate higher satisfaction (Olson et al., 1985). This measure taps one aspect of marital adjustment, one of the factors affecting recovery from stress or crisis.

Data Analysis

A variety of statistical analyses were used, depending on the type of question being asked and the measure scale of the variables being investigated. Most commonly *t*-tests were used to compare means by group (paired *t*-tests when within couple analyses were conducted). In addition, chi square analyses and other nonparametric tests were used as appropriate, as were Pearson product-moment correlations.

Chapter 4

Inmate Family Coping

INMATE AND WIFE STRESS AND COPING

The first research question posed was, "How well do inmates and their wives cope with the experience of incarceration?" While numerous aspects of the prison experience may be perceived by inmates as stressful, the most common type of stress reported by this group of inmates was family concerns, mentioned by 82%. All but one of the wives interviewed reported that the experience of being the wife of someone in prison is stressful. When asked to indicate the most stressful aspect of their husband being imprisoned, the most common answer, reported by 38%, is "everything." Wives who were able to be more specific reported that tight or uncertain finances created stress for them (26%) and that dealing with their children (17%) and being a single parent (17%) caused them stress. These findings are consistent with literature on the effects of incarceration on wives discussed in Chapter 2.

Two sources of data pertain to how inmates and their wives cope with that stress: questions posed in our interview and Family Crisis Oriented Personal Evaluation Scales (F-COPES) responses. According to the wives' responses to our questions, the most commonly used means of coping with their husbands' incarceration were family support and faith or religion, each reported by 26%; their children, who helped to keep them going, reported by 23%; and talking to and visiting the inmate, reported by 21%. Thirteen percent also mentioned that staying busy with school or work was helpful. A significant number of inmates (40%) also reported that prison work or school was helpful in coping, as were exercise and sports (33%). Writing letters to significant others (13%) and visits (10%) were also mentioned by inmates as factors that were helpful in dealing with the incarceration experience.

F-COPES scores measure the extent to which husbands and wives use a variety of problem-solving strategies to cope with difficult situations. Means for the F-COPES total score and five subscales are reported for inmates and their wives in Table 4.1. Based on norms derived from two large samples of husbands, wives, and adolescents (Olson et al., 1985), the mean F-COPES total for inmates would place them at the seventieth percentile, and the wives' mean would put them at the sixty-second percentile. The means for both inmates and wives are well above the means obtained by McCubbin on the large national sample.

Turning to the subscale scores, on Acquiring Social Support, inmates placed at the thirty-fifth percentile, while wives were at the thirty-seventh percentile. The means for both were slightly

Table 4.1
Mean F-COPES Scores for Inmates and Wives

	Inmates			Wives		
	M	SD	N	M	SD	N
Social support	24.54	7.72	59	25.68	6.80	34
Reframing	34.10	5.36	59	33.08	5.66	36
Spiritual support	14.49	4.38	61	16.68	3.46	34
Mobilizing for help	12.57	4.18	60	13.39	3.41	36
Passive appraisal	14.54	4.09	61	14.62	3.44	37
Total	99.93	14.34	61	99.63	20.47	38

below the means obtained by McCubbin. Regarding Reframing, both inmates and wives scored well above the mean and placed at the eighty-third and seventy-seventh percentiles, respectively. On Seeking Spiritual Support, inmates scored below the mean, at the twenty-sixth percentile, whereas wives scored at the mean and achieved the fortieth percentile. Regarding the subscale Mobilizing the Family to Acquire and Accept Help, both inmates and wives scored slightly above the mean, at the sixty-ninth and fifty-seventh percentiles, respectively. Finally, on Passive Appraisal, both inmates and wives scored well above the mean, at the ninety-seventh percentile.

In general, these findings indicate that our inmates and wives were coping very well with the difficult experience of incarceration and were remarkably similar to each other in terms of the types of coping strategies they employed. On the basis of the subscale scores, both spouses were most likely to rely on Passive Appraisal and Reframing and least likely to employ Acquiring Social Support and Seeking Spiritual Support as coping strategies, compared to others who have taken the F-COPES. Enhanced coping would entail more reaching out to significant others for social support and greater reliance on organized religion and the solace it can offer.

Coping by Ethnicity

Inmate and wife F-COPES scores were examined separately by ethnicity, combining African-Americans and Latinos into one group due to the limited sample sizes. These scores are shown in Table 4.2. Nonwhite inmates scored significantly higher ($t = 1.88$, $df = 58$, $p < .002$) on the F-COPES total ($\overline{X} = 101.28$) than white inmates ($\overline{X} = 99.31$), indicating higher coping overall. However, there were no significant differences on any of the specific subscales. Among the wives, there was a trend for white wives to score higher on total coping than nonwhite wives ($t = 1.83$, $df = 33$, $p < .082$). No differences were observed on the subscale scores. However, examination of the total coping scores suggests that the

Table 4.2
Mean F-COPES Scores for Inmates and Wives, by Ethnicity

| | Inmates | | | | | | Wives | | | | | |
| | White | | | Nonwhite | | | White | | | Nonwhite | | |
	M	SD	N	M	SD	N	M	SD	N	M	SD	N
Social support	24.42	9.38	12	24.84	7.31	45	28.50	8.47	8	25.09	5.78	23
Reframing	34.54	4.67	13	34.48	4.48	44	34.33	5.68	9	32.33	5.96	24
Spiritual support	12.54	5.06	13	15.33	3.78	46	15.63	3.85	8	17.05	3.43	22
Mobilizing for help	12.62	4.19	13	12.69	4.16	45	13.67	3.87	9	13.21	3.27	24
Passive appraisal	15.46	3.13	13	14.30	4.28	46	14.22	3.70	9	14.68	3.60	24
Total	99.31	18.97	11	101.28	10.07	41	105.44	12.78	9	97.92	23.30	25

differences, while statistically significant, were not of great magnitude in either case.

F-COPES scores can also be compared in terms of how the different ethnic groups compare on established norms for the total and five subscales. Among inmates there were no differences by ethnicity in scores on Acquiring Social Support (both at the fortieth percentile), Reframing (both at the eighty-fifth percentile), Mobilizing for Help (both at the sixty-fourth percentile), and Passive Appraisal (both at the ninety-seventh percentile). However, on Spiritual Support, nonwhite inmates scored at the fortieth percentile in contrast to white inmates who scored only at the sixteenth percentile. This is consistent with work on the black and Hispanic communities that indicated the importance of organized religion as a coping strategy and source of support (London and Devore, 1988). Finally, the F-COPES total was similar with white inmates scoring at the seventieth percentile and nonwhites at the seventy-fifth.

More notable differences were observed on F-COPES scores between white and nonwhite wives. Only on Passive Appraisal were scores virtually the same, with both groups scoring at the ninety-seventh percentile. Mobilizing for Help scores were similar, with white wives at the sixty-sixth percentile and nonwhite wives at the sixtieth. However, white wives scored noticeably higher than black and Latino wives on Acquiring Social Support (fifty-fourth versus thirty-second percentile) and Reframing (eighty-fourth versus seventy-first percentile). Given the tendency toward heavy reliance on extended families in minority communities, this finding is rather unexpected (Boyd-Franklin, 1989; Hill, 1972; Sanchez-Ayendez, 1988). The reverse pattern was observed for Spiritual Support, where nonwhite wives scored higher (fifty-seventh versus thirty-sixth percentile), again consistent with literature on coping in the African-American and Hispanic communities, where religion plays an important role. Overall, however, white women scored higher on total coping, placing at the eighty-first percentile, in contrast to nonwhite women who were at the fifty-eighth percentile.

To better understand the patterns of coping across inmates and wives, regardless of ethnicity, it may be helpful to examine the individual items from which the subscales are composed. The items that compose the Passive Appraisal subscale reflect a sense of resignation, a sense that the solutions to problems are not under one's control, that things are instead controlled by fate (for example, "Knowing luck plays a big part in how well we are able to solve family problems"; "Believing that if we wait long enough the problem will go away"; "Feeling that no matter what we do to prepare, we will have difficulty handling problems"). Endorsement of such items to a large extent reflects the reality of the situations in which these couples find themselves and explains why inmates and wives, irrespective of ethnic background, score so high on this dimension.

In contrast, Reframing suggests an acceptance of the inevitability of problems but at the same time a belief in one's ability to solve them, a self-confidence that one can successfully confront difficulties (for example, "Accepting stressful events as a fact of life"; "Facing the problem head on and trying to get solutions right away"; "Believing that we can handle our own problems").

Both Reframing and Passive Appraisal can be considered to be cognitive strategies that indicate how a person perceives problems and their potential solutions rather than the actions he/she takes. As such, they are available to virtually anyone, regardless of their circumstance. In contrast, Acquiring Social Support and Mobilizing the Family to Acquire and Accept Help are more behavioral or action-oriented strategies that describe what people actually do when confronted by problems. Several of the Social Support items in particular are not even feasible for inmates, for example "Sharing problems with neighbors," "Receiving gifts and favors from neighbors," and "Doing things with relatives." In addition, several of the items composing the Mobilizing the Family subscale may be relatively unacceptable in the African-American and Latino communities where there are strong norms that inhibit sharing problems and seeking their solutions outside the extended family (Sanchez-Ayendez, 1988). Examples of such items are "Seeking assistance from community agencies and programs designed to help families in our situation" and "Seeking information and advice from the family doctor." Families as poor as many of these may never have had a family physician and are forced to rely instead on Medicaid and public clinics.

It is not suprising that ethnic differences on Seeking Spiritual Support were observed for both husbands and wives (although they were not large enough to achieve statistical significance, in part because of small sample sizes for white inmates and wives). Reliance on religion and faith in God have been traditional means of coping commonly used in the minority communities (Boyd-Franklin, 1989; London and Devore, 1988; Sanchez-Ayendez, 1988).

SUPPORT TO WIVES

One factor that could be of great use to wives as they struggle to maintain their lives on the outside is the support they receive from others. We know from the Acquiring Social Support subscale that white and nonwhite wives score only at the fifty-fourth and thirty-second percentiles, respectively, on this coping strategy, and we sought to better understand the wives' use (or lack thereof) of this means of coping. Accordingly, the second research question addresses this and asks: "What kinds of supports are received by wives and how adequate are they to meet their needs?"

All thirty-nine wives reported having regular, in-person contact with their extended families. For almost half, this contact was daily (44%); 15% saw their families two to three times per week, 10% weekly, 10% every two weeks, and 20% monthly or less. Thus, more than two-thirds have direct contact with their extended families at least once a week. This is not suprising given that most of the sample is nonwhite, and closeness to extended family is a strong norm in the African-American and Hispanic communities (Hill, 1972; Sanchez-Ayendez, 1988). Although ethnic differences in frequency of contact with extended family were not statistically significant, it is worth noting that half of the nonwhite wives saw their extended families on a daily basis, in contrast to one-third of white wives.

Perhaps more important than how often they saw their families is how helpful their families were in providing practical or emotional support. Almost two-thirds (64%) of wives reported that their families provided help, most commonly money, babysitting, and other forms of concrete assistance. In addition, over three-quarters (77%) indicated that their families provided emotional support as well, in the form of moral support and listening, as well as visits and calls. These are coping strategies highly touted in the literature as enhancing overall coping effectiveness (McCubbin, 1979). However, 24% said that there were things they wished their families were doing, such as being more more understanding of them and more supportive to their husbands. No ethnic differences were evident on these variables.

All wives except one also indicated that they have face-to-face contact with the inmate's family; for 18% this contact was daily, 8% weekly, 16% every two weeks, 24% monthly, and 29% less than monthly. This contact was weekly or more often for only one-quarter of the wives, compared to the two-thirds who saw their own families that frequently. Perhaps more significant is the fact that only 41% received any practical assistance from their husband's family, most often money, babysitting, or occasionally a place to live.

However, although 78% of white wives and 58% of nonwhite wives reported receiving emotional support, almost half of both groups reported that there were things their husband's family could be doing but was not. These things most often consisted of visiting the inmate, staying in closer contact with the children, providing financial assistance, and being more understanding of the wife. The findings regarding assistance received from extended families are congruent with what other researchers have found. Although family members help, this assistance is not sufficient to meet all of wives' needs and more help is received from the wife's family than the husband's (Morris, 1965; Schneller, 1975a; Schwartz and Weintraub, 1974; Swan, 1981).

Finally, many wives also received support or assistance from neighbors. Seventy-eight percent of white wives and 58% of nonwhite wives said that they were close to their neighbors, seeing them at least weekly. However, only about one-third of wives received any practical support from neighbors, most commonly such things as babysitting, loans of money, or the use of their phone.

INMATE-WIFE COMMUNICATION

Another potentially important aspect of coping is communication between inmates and their wives. We asked: "How extensive is communication between inmates and their wives, and what forms does it take?"

Virtually all the inmates we interviewed (95%) reported that they telephoned their wives (inmates in New York State are not permitted to receive phone calls and, thus, must call collect to speak to their families, which is expensive for the families). Almost two-thirds (64%) reported phone conversations more than once a week, with an additional 17% reporting weekly conversations; only 17% spoke to their wives less often than once a week. The most common topic of conversation, reported by over half of the inmates, was their children. An additional 25% talked about how their wives were, 24% discussed the future, 15% talked about how they were, and 5% discussed how they miss and/or love their wives. No ethnic differences existed regarding telephone communication.

Similarly, virtually all of the inmates also reported that they spoke to their children by telephone. Over half have such conversations more than once a week (56%), with another 16% talking to them weekly. Only 28% spoke to their children less often than once a week. Whereas three-quarters of nonwhite inmates talked to their children at least weekly, only half of white inmates spoke to them that frequently. The majority of all inmates reported that their telephone conversations have a positive effect on their relationships with their families. Thus, it can be concluded that verbal communication between inmates and their wives and children is not only regular and frequent but also primarily positive.

The vast majority, 88% of the sample, of inmates also wrote letters to their wives. Those who write said they do so with great regularity: Over half (56%) wrote more than once a week and 24% wrote weekly; the remainder wrote less often. Three-quarters of the inmates also indicated that they wrote letters to their children. Over half of those who wrote to their children did so at least once a week, while 42% said they wrote less often. There were no ethnic differences in frequency of writing to wives or children.

Wives concurred with inmates' reports regarding verbal and written communication. The vast majority (95%) spoke to their husbands by phone. Almost two-thirds (62%) of those who speak by phone do so more than once a week; another 24% spoke to their husbands weekly; only 14% estimated that they talked to their husbands less often than weekly. There is a trend for white wives to speak to their husbands more frequently (78% more than once a week, compared to 54% of nonwhite wives; no white wives spoke less than weekly, whereas 21% of nonwhite wives spoke less than weekly). This difference may be related to economic resources, insofar as wives must bear the total financial burden of such conversations, and nonwhite wives were twice as likely to be on Public Assistance as white wives.

The most common topic of phone conversation, reported by 65% of the wives, was their children. Half also discussed how things were going at home, one-third talked about what the inmate was doing, and 22% discussed what they will do once the inmate was released. A major difference was observed between inmates and wives regarding the perceived effect of phone calls on the relationship. Whereas the majority of inmates felt the calls have a positive impact, 76% of both white and nonwhite wives reported that such calls had a negative effect. Perhaps the calls reminded them of how hard their life on the outside is, or the inmate made requests of her that created real hardships, as Fishman (1990) reported. These requests might include such things as expensive athletic shoes or clothing that the wife cannot afford on her limited budget.

The majority of wives also wrote letters to their husbands, although not as many or as frequently as the inmates wrote to them. Of the 69% who wrote, 39% wrote more than once a week and 25% wrote weekly. The most frequent topics of these letters are similar to those discussed on the telephone: children (32%), what has been happening in their lives (32%), how much they love and miss the inmate (29%), and their jobs (14%). There were no ethnic differences in letter writing to husbands.

FACTORS ASSOCIATED WITH COPING

Although both inmates and their wives as a whole were coping well with the experience of incarceration, there was variability in how well they dealt with the experience. Thus, we were interested in identifying what factors appeared to be associated with more effective coping ability and asked: "What factors are associated with enhanced coping on the part of inmates and wives?" To explore this question we computed Pearson product-moment correlation coefficients, separately for inmates and wives, between F-COPES scores and a variety of other variables we thought might be related to coping. In addition, the coping of first-time inmates and their wives was compared with that of couples who had previously experienced incarceration and thus had more opportunity to develop coping skills.

For inmates, we suspected that coping might relate to the length of time in prison, the frequency of communication with wives and children (including by phone, in letters, and in-person visits), and their perceived closeness to their wives and children. Significant correlations between measures of coping and other variables are depicted in Table 4.3.

Positive relationships were found between total coping and Reframing and perceived closeness to one's wife; Reframing was also positively associated with the frequency of writing to one's wife. Passive Appraisal was negatively associated with perceived closeness to children. In addition, for those who had participated in the FRP, Seeking Spiritual Support was positively related to the number of FRP visits the inmate had experienced.

These findings suggest that inmates who perceive themselves to be closer to their wives and have greater contact with them are able to cope more effectively with being in prison. The negative correlation between Passive Appraisal and perceived closeness to children suggests that inmates who perceive themselves to be closer to their children have more difficulty simply accepting the reality of their incarceration without reactivity.

For wives, we speculated that coping would be related to the adequacy of support, as well as frequency of communication with the inmate, perceived closeness, number of FRP visits, adequacy of income, and length of marriage. Several significant correlations were obtained, as well as several marginally significant relationships that will be reported as trends, taking into account the small sample size for wives. These relationships are shown in Table 4.3.

There are two marginally significant, negative correlations with total F-COPES score: an association with the frequency of writing

Table 4.3
Significant Correlations Between Coping Measures and Other Variables

F-COPES scores	Other variables	Correlation	p	N
Inmates				
Total	Closeness to wife	.31	.008	59
Reframing	Closeness to wife	.50	.0001	57
Reframing	Frequency of writing to wife	.24	.05	53
Passive appraisal	Closeness to children	-.29	.02	58
Spiritual support	Number of FRP visits	.30	.05	33
Wives				
Total	Frequency of writing to inmate	-.30	.067	27
Total	His family not helping	.26	.065	36
Social support	Frequency of talking to inmate	.28	.063	32
Social support	Frequency of seeing inmate's family	-.27	.063	34
Social support	Frequency of seeing neighbors	.34	.055	23
Social support	Frequency of neighbors helping	-.24	.089	32
Reframing	Emotional support from own family	-.33	.03	36
Reframing	Frequency of seeing neighbors	.54	.003	25

Table 4.3 (continued)

F-COPES scores	Other variables	Correlation	p	N
Wives				
Reframing	Frequency of talking to inmate	.23	.094	34
Spiritual support	Frequency of seeing inmate's family	-.34	.03	33
Spiritual support	Length of marriage	-.43	.057	15
Passive appraisal	Frequency of talking to inmate	-.40	.008	35
Passive appraisal	Frequency of help from neighbors	.32	.03	35
Passive appraisal	Adequacy of income	.23	.083	37
Passive appraisal	Frequency of writing	-.29	.077	26

to the inmate and with reporting that there are things that the inmate's family is not doing to help. The Social Support subscale is related marginally to several variables: positively to frequency of talking to the inmate and frequency of seeing neighbors; and negatively with seeing the inmate's family and neighbors helping. Wives' Reframing is negatively correlated with receiving emotional support from her own family and positively associated with seeing her neighbors, and (marginally) to the frequency of talking to the inmate. A negative relationship is also found between Seeking Spiritual Support and frequency of seeing the inmate's family and (marginally) with length of marriage. Finally, wives' Passive Appraisal is negatively correlated with frequency of talking to the inmate and positively associated with receiving help from neighbors. Passive Appraisal is also marginally associated with the adequacy of income and negatively with the frequency of writing.

Although one cannot determine direction of effects from correlations, several tentative conclusions can be drawn from the observed relationships. First, it appears that wives are likely to turn to nonfamily sources of support when the inmate's family provides little assistance to them. That is, wives are more likely to acquire Social Support and seek Spiritual Support when they have limited contact with the inmate's family, perhaps as a compensation for that lack of contact. More frequent verbal communication with the inmate is also associated with enhanced ability to seek Social Support and to use Reframing and active coping strategies, whereas low verbal and written communication with the inmate is related to Passive Appraisal and a sense of helplessness or resignation.

Coping of First-Timers versus Recidivists

F-COPES scores of inmates and wives who had experienced a previous incarceration of the husband were compared with those of couples who were coping with this crisis for the first time among those couples where we could obtain this information. There were twenty-one inmates who had not been to prison previously and nineteen who had been incarcerated at an earlier time. Fifteen wives were coping with their husbands' incarceration for the first time, in contrast to ten who had dealt with it previously.

Among the wives, the F-COPES total was significantly higher for those who had previously experienced incarceration ($t = 2.16$, $df = 25$, $p < .01$), indicating more effective coping. Although none of the subscale scores were significantly different, the largest difference occurred in the Reframing score. In addition, the number of years their husband had served in prison was modestly associated with overall coping among wives [$r(36) = .24$, $p < .076$]. The effect of previous incarceration is even more pronounced on inmates: Those who had been in prison before cope significantly better ($t = 2.42$, $df = 39$, $p < .0001$). Again, no differences were observed on the specific subscales. These findings indicate that having previous experience with this type of crisis is advantageous in coping more effectively with its effects, consistent with stress family theory (Hansen and Hill, 1964).

Summary

The data validate that prison is a stressful experience for both inmates and their wives. The most common source of stress for inmates was family concerns, whereas wives were most concerned with tight finances, handling their children, and being a single parent. Inmates reported prison employment and educational opportunities, exercise, writing letters to loved ones, and visits as means of coping. Wives rely most on family support, religious faith, their children, talking to and visiting the inmate, and staying busy to cope with the stress of an incarcerated spouse.

As compared with established norms, the inmates and wives studied here were coping quite well, irrespective of ethnic affiliation. Inmates and wives most commonly used Reframing and Passive Appraisal as coping strategies. Inmates and white wives were least likely to rely on Seeking Spiritual Support, in contrast to black wives who scored lowest on Acquiring Social Support as a means of coping.

Regarding support to wives, a high level of contact with one's own extended family was reported, and most of these families were said to provide practical assistance as well as emotional support. However, a sizeable subgroup indicated that there were additional things they wished their families were doing. Much less contact was reported with the inmate's family of origin, as well as less practical assistance. Although these families, too, provided emotional support, many wives reported that they wished the inmate's family would do more to be of assistance.

Another source of support to wives was communication between them and their spouses. Telephone communication between the inmate, his wife, and his children was regular and frequent, as was letter writing. However, the inmates rated these communications more positively in terms of their effect on the marital relationship than did their wives.

For inmates, having more frequent contact with their wives and feeling closer to them was associated with more effective coping. Predictors of coping among wives were more complex, with more frequent communication related to some forms of coping, and less frequent communication associated with greater reliance on other coping strategies. Finally, overall coping was significantly higher among both inmates and wives who have experienced incarceration previously, as predicted by the family stress and coping literature.

Chapter 5

Family Relations

QUALITY OF COUPLE RELATIONSHIPS

Because incarceration is thought to have a negative impact on marital relationships we were interested in determining the quality of the marital relationship of the inmates and wives in our sample. How well do these couples function as marital units? Specifically, we asked several questions, including: "How cohesive, adaptable, and satisfied with the relationship are these couples? How close do they feel to one another? How is decision making distributed between the spouses, and has that changed over time?" Finally, we were also interested in whether or not any of these variables appeared to be affected by ethnicity.

Cohesion and Adaptability

Table 5.1 depicts mean Cohesion and Adaptability scores for inmates and wives based on the FACES III instrument. Cohesion means for both inmates and wives place them on the boundary between the "separated" and "connected" categories of the Circumplex Model, exactly in the middle of the normal range based on Olson et al.'s (1985) research. This indicates that these couples are emotionally bonded to and supportive of one another to an appropriate degree. That is, they are neither overly involved with one another, nor are they overly distant (Olson et al., 1985).

Table 5.1
Mean Scores on Measures of Family Functioning

	Inmates			Wives		
	M	SD	N	M	SD	N
Cohesion	40.85	6.50	61	41.22	5.25	37
Adaptability	32.19	6.68	59	31.87	7.70	39
Family satisfaction	8.00	8.85	56	13.33	12.52	36
Perceived closeness	6.10	1.52	59	6.33	1.22	39
Decision making, now	20.90	3.45	52	24.13	4.40	39
Decision making, before	16.98	3.74	60	20.70	4.81	37

Adaptability means are depicted in Table 5.1. The scores for both inmates and wives place them at the low end of the "chaotic" range (just above the "flexible" category), based on norms for the *Family Adaptability and Cohesion Evaluation Scales* (FACES III). Insofar as adaptability measures how flexible the family is in dealing with change, this score suggests possible problems related to "family power (assertiveness, control, discipline), negotiation style, role relationships, and relationship rules" (Olson et al., 1985, 4). Lack of consistency in family leadership and discipline, ineffective negotiation, and poor communication are possible problems in these kinds of families.

Perusal of the individual adaptability items offers some insight regarding both strengths and difficulties. Among wives, the highest scores were on items pertaining to compromising when problems arose in the family, flexibility in handling differences, trying new ways of dealing with problems, and making decisions jointly as a couple. On these items the mean scores were at or near 4.00, which is anchored at "frequently" on the five point scale. On the other hand, problems occurred with regard to leadership in the marriage, performance of household tasks and chores, and rules in the marriage, where the low scores suggest lack of flexibility or confusion.

There was remarkable similarity on these items as they were evaluated by inmates. Again, strength was observed in compromising when problems arose and in joint decision making, whereas difficulties appeared in the areas of marital leadership, agreement on roles, and flexibility of rules. Thus, there was congruence between inmates and wives about the confusion and lack of flexibility regarding leadership, marital role performance, and relationship rules. In a society where men are still expected to be the head of the household and family roles are still largely gender-based, this confusion may reflect conflict or lack of agreement on these issues in families who are coping with an incarcerated husband.

Family Satisfaction

Family satisfaction is measured in the Circumplex Model by computing the difference between each family member's perception of how the family actually functions versus how he or she thinks it should function ideally, higher scores indicating lower satisfaction with family life. Means on family satisfaction can be found in Table 5.1. Unfortunately, norms regarding family satisfaction are not currently available so we can only speculate as to the meaning of these scores and whether or not they differ from what would be expected in a more normal sample. However, by inspection it can be seen that the mean discrepancy for wives is notably greater than that for inmates, and that the wives' family satisfaction scores are more variable than the husbands'.

These findings suggest that wives are less satisfied with the couple relationship than are their husbands. This is consistent with the literature indicating that male inmates are more satisfied with their marital relationships than their wives and to some extent may distort or deny problems that exist (Showalter and Jones, 1980).

For example, Hannon et al. (1984) noted that "expression of marital satisfaction by prisoners may be a deliberate misrepresentation based on their need for outside contacts" (258).

The finding that wives reported higher marital dissatisfaction than inmates may also reflect the fact that inmates have more to gain from being married than do their wives. Whereas inmates obtain a support system by being married, their wives must come to terms with a demanding burden that imposes restrictions on their lives and that implies major obligations such as visiting and financial support (Rieger, 1973). At the same time, wives of inmates may gain little of practical value from their husbands (although there may be significant emotional attachment), because prison prevents meaningful reciprocation in a relationship that is defined by mutuality (Holt and Miller, 1972). In addition, wives are limited in their ability to form other romantic relationships.

HUSBAND-WIFE CLOSENESS

Means on perceived closeness scores are depicted in Table 5.1. It can be seen that perceived closeness for both inmates and their wives is quite high (seven is the highest value on the scale) with little variation. Thus, we can conclude that inmates feel quite close to their wives, and that wives also feel extremely close to their husbands, despite the husband being incarcerated. These results are consistent with the FACES cohesion scores indicating a high degree of emotional bonding among these couples.

DECISION MAKING

A series of questions were posed regarding how decision making is distributed between husbands and wives, both currently and prior to the husbands' incarceration. Responses were coded on a five point scale as follows: (1) "husband always," (2) "husband most of the time," (3) "husband and wife equally," (4) "wife most of the time," and (5) "wife always." Categories 1 and 2 are combined, as are 4 and 5, to simplify presentation of these findings.

Preincarceration Decision Making

Prior to incarceration, husbands reported that decision making varies by domain. In regard to children, a domain in which wives traditionally have had greater influence than husbands, inmates reported themselves to have significant influence. On "when children should be disciplined," 44% of inmates said they made these decisions all or most of the time and 42% said such decisions were made equally with their wives, while only 14% said their wives made these decisions all or most of the time. Somewhat less husband influence was reported in relation to "when children are old enough to try new things": 31% said they decided this all or most of the time, 47% said it was decided equally, and only 22% said it was decided by their wives all or most of the time.

The reports of wives regarding these child-related decisions are similar, although wives reported greater influence for themselves in both areas. On "when children should be disciplined," 28% of the wives said that their husbands made such decisions all or most of the time, 42% said such decisions were made equally, and 30% said they decided about child discipline all or most of the time. Regarding "when children are old enough to try new things," 23% of wives said their husbands decided on such matters all or most of the time, 48% said it was decided equally, and 29% said they had greater influence than their husband in this domain.

Financial decisions are in a domain in which husbands have traditionally had greater influence than wives. Regarding "when to make major purchases," 30% of the inmates reported that they made such decisions all or most of the time, half (49%) reported that these decisions were made equally between their wives and themselves, and 21% said that their wives made decisions about this all or most of the time. Interestingly, wives were reported by husbands to have a great deal of influence over "how much to spend" on various items: Only 8% of inmates said they have greater influence over this decision, 48% reported that these decisions were made equally, and 44% said their wives made such decisions all or most of the time.

Regarding "when to make major purchases," 28% of the wives reported that their husbands made these decisions all or most of the time, 51% said that such decisions were made equally, and 21% said they made decisions about this all or most of the time. This distribution of responses is almost identical to that reported by the inmates. With regard to "how much to spend," 26% of the wives reported that their husbands had greater influence in this area, 49% reported equal decision making, and 35% reported that they made these decisions all or most of the time. Husbands reported that their wives have somewhat greater influence in this area than the wives said they have.

Questions were also asked regarding each spouse's job (or whether or not the wife should be employed). According to husbands, the modal response was that each partner made decisions regarding his or her own job all or most of the time (77% for the husband's job and 55% for the wife's job), followed by the couple having an equal say in job-related decisions (20% in regard to the husband's job and 32% in regard to the wife's job). Only 3% of the inmates reported that their wives have greater influence over the inmate's job than they themselves do, whereas 13% of inmates said they have greater influence over their wives' job-related decisions than their wives do.

Wives' responses in relation to their husbands' jobs were quite congruent with their husbands' responses: 80% said their husbands decided on these matters all or most of the time, 15% said the partners have an equal say in these matters, and 5% said they have a greater say than their husbands do in relation to decisions about his job. In regard to their own jobs, 64% of wives said they make decisions in this arena all or most of the time, 24% said these decisions were made equally, and 12% said their husbands have more influence over their job-related decisions.

Decision Making During Incarceration

The same questions were asked of the sample regarding decision making at the time of the interview, while the husband was incarcerated. In regard to "when children should be disciplined,"

86% of the inmates said their wives made these decisions all or most of the time, and 14% said such decisions were made equally. No inmates said they had greater influence than their wives over decisions about child discipline. Similarly, the vast majority of wives (76%) said that they made decisions about when to discipline their children all or most of the time, whereas 18% said these decisions were made equally. However, 6% said their husbands had greater influence over these decisions.

Regarding "when children are old enough to try new things," again the modal response for inmates (43%) was that their wives made these decisions all or most of the time. But almost one-third (32%) of inmates said such decisions were made equally, and one-quarter reported that they made decisions about these matters all or most of the time. Thus, in child-related matters, wives have the most influence over decisions, but husbands still retain some influence, especially regarding when children are old enough to do new things.

According to inmates, decisions about "when to make major purchases" were made exclusively or primarily by wives in almost half of the sample (48%), but were made equally by 43%. Nine percent of the inmates said they made these decisions all or most of the time. However, wives appear to have greater influence over "how much to spend": 77% of the inmates said their wives made such decisions all or most of the time, while decisions were made equally in 22% of the couples.

Wives generally concurred regarding financial decision making during their husbands' incarceration. Half reported that they had greater say over when to make major purchases, while 43% reported equal decision making, and only 3% indicated that their husbands had more influence in this area. Like their husbands, they reported much greater influence for themselves with regard to how much to spend on household purchases: 90% said they made all or most of these decisions, 8% said these decisions were shared, and 3% said their husbands primarily made these decisions.

Regarding the wife's job, 78% of the inmates reported that she made these decisions all or most of the time, while 20% reported equal decision making in this area. However, 90% of wives said they made these decisions for the most part, with the remainder saying decisions regarding their jobs were made jointly.

In conclusion, for each decision arena, inmates and their wives agreed that during the husband's incarceration the modal decision-making pattern is for wives to have greater influence. This is reflected in the scores on the four decision-making scales that were created, one each for husbands and wives before and during incarceration. These scales were developed to reduce the data and take into account decision-making influence across all the arenas and, in addition, to get an overall picture of decision making. The totals (see Table 5.1) were created by summing the answers to each of the items separately for husbands and wives at each point in time. Given the values for the individual items (where one equals husband always and five equals wife always), higher scores represent more wife influence. The means indicate that inmate and wife agreement that wives' influence in decision making increases from the pre-incarceration period to the time of the interview during incarceration.

However, inmates continue to exert some influence over decisions in all areas except the wife's job, especially with regard to when the children are old enough to begin new things and when to purchase major items. This clearly represents a shift from the patterns that were more prevalent before the husband was incarcerated, when the modal pattern for most decisions was one of equally shared or husband-dominated decision making, except with regard to the wife's job. Although it is not known how the distribution of decision making is perceived by these husbands and wives, the pattern observed appears functional based on the circumstances in which these families find themselves, with the likelihood of the husband returning to the family in the future.

ETHNICITY AND FAMILY FUNCTIONING

Cohesion and adaptability, family satisfaction, husband-wife and father-child closeness, and decision making were examined by ethnicity, comparing scores for white and nonwhite inmates and wives. Very few differences were observed as a function of ethnicity.[1] Among inmates, white husbands reported feeling significantly closer to their wives than did nonwhite husbands [$t = 1.88$, $df = 58$, $p < .002$]. However, the means for both groups of inmates were greater than six on a seven point scale, so the difference is not terribly meaningful despite being statistically significant. In addition, nonwhite wives perceived that their children felt closer to their fathers than did white wives [$t = 1.71$, $df = 31$, $p < .042$]. Again, the means were quite close, $\overline{X} = 6.58$ for nonwhite wives and $\overline{X} = 5.67$ for white wives. No ethnic differences were found for cohesion or adaptability, family satisfaction, or decision making.

FATHER-CHILD RELATIONSHIPS

Although neither formal research questions nor hypotheses were formulated regarding how inmates viewed their roles as fathers and interacted with their children, a series of questions were included in the inmate interview to explore these areas.

In response to the question, "How important is being a father to you now?" almost no variability in the responses was found: 92% of the inmates answered "very important." Only one admitted that it was "not too important," and none said that it was only "somewhat important." This may to some extent reflect social desirability insofar as many of these inmates are undoubtedly sophisticated enough to know that it is not socially acceptable today to admit lack of investment in the father role. However, such awareness would be noteworthy in a marginal population such as this one.

In addition, inmate responses to the question, "What does being a father mean?" suggest an awareness of essential elements of the father role despite the fact of being incarcerated. For example, one-third reported that being a father means responsibility, and one-quarter said it means helping and advising their children. Others said that it means watching children grow (10%), being somebody who cares (8%), and setting an example (7%).

Thus, it is not surprising that the inmates feel very close to their children. Their mean response to the question, "How close do you feel to your children?" (on a seven point scale where one is "very distant" and seven is "very close") was 6.17, with relatively little variability (SD = 1.58). Only ten inmates evaluated their closeness at the midpoint of the scale or lower. These findings contrast somewhat with those of Lanier (1987), whose New York State inmate fathers reported high levels of closeness prior to incarceration, but only half of whom reported feeling very close to their children while in prison. Only 30% of his sample was currently married to the mothers of their children, as all these inmates were, and this may explain the lack of closeness reported.

The high level of perceived closeness reported here may be a reflection of the frequent communication in the form of telephone calls and letters between inmates and their children, as well as their intense need to feel close to their significant others. In addition, most inmates see their children frequently during visits. Seventeen percent see their children on a weekly basis, 12% see them every two weeks, 33% see them monthly, and 34% see them every two months or less often. This distribution is quite similar to what Lanier (1987) found: 64% of the inmates studied here saw their children monthly or less, as did 70% of Lanier's fathers. Hairston (1990), too, reports that 62% of her sample of Southern married, male inmate fathers saw their children regularly. Thus, these regular forms of contact may enable these inmates to maintain feelings of closeness to their children despite being incarcerated.

SUMMARY

The findings reported here indicate that inmates and their wives are emotionally close and supportive of one another. This conclusion is supported by the FACES III cohesion scores as well as by the inmates' and wives' self-reported ratings of their closeness to one another. However, not surprisingly, attempting to maintain a marital relationship under the stressful conditions of incarceration is challenging, and inmates and their wives had difficulty with role flexibility and marital leadership, as indicated by the FACES III adaptability scores. Consistent with the incarceration and family life literature, wives were less satisfied with their marital relationships than were their inmate husbands.

Prior to incarceration inmates and their wives reported equally shared or husband dominated decision making regarding child-related matters. The findings also indicate agreement that husbands and wives had equal influence over how and when money was spent for household purchases prior to incarceration. Although such a pattern of shared decision making might be expected among African-American couples, where egalitarian marriages are relatively common, it was somewhat surprising to find this degree of joint decision making among the white inmate couples, especially in light of their likely social class backgrounds. Caution must be used in interpreting these findings because of their retrospective nature. In addition, responses may have been influenced by social desirability or the tendency to idealize their marriages.

Wives' decision-making powers significantly shifted following their husbands' incarceration based on both the individual items and the overall decision-making scale scores. Respondents agreed that at the time of the study wives had the major influence in making decisions about the children's discipline. However, husbands and wives agreed that inmates continued to have a major impact on when children were old enough to try new things. There was also agreement that while wives' influence in financial matters increased, inmates continued to have influence over when major purchases would be made.

There was a strong consensus among inmates that their fathering role was very important to them, and most appeared to have a reasonable appreciation for what being a good father entailed. This investment in the father role was reflected in the uniformly high scores on perceived closeness to their children. Such closeness may be supported by the frequent communication between inmates and their children, which included telephoning, writing letters, and visiting by their children. Incredibly, 62% of the inmates in our sample received visits from their children at least on a monthly basis. This may also reflect the wives' strength of commitment to maintaining family ties.

It can be concluded that despite the extreme hardship that incarceration places on a family, both husbands and wives were functioning remarkably well in terms of their closeness to one another, the adaptability of their relationships, and the quality of their decision making. This may be attributed to the substantial investment made in maintaining family life by these couples, although there are obvious limits to how much can be done to maintain family life from behind prison walls in the absence of regular, day-to-day interaction among family members.

NOTE

1. African-Americans and Latinos were aggregated into one group, since neither group was large enough to examine separately. This makes some assumptions about their similarity to one another that may be unwarranted and may obscure differences between either group and white inmates and wives.

Chapter 6

Findings: Family Reunion Program

TYPICAL FAMILY REUNION VISIT

Inmates

Now we turn to the Family Reunion Program (FRP) and what the experience of conjugal visits was like for the inmates and wives who participated in it. At a very basic level we wanted to know about the frequency of visits, what occurred on a typical visit, and how it was experienced by the participants. Thus we asked: "How often do Family Reunion visits take place and what occurs during a typical visit?"

Thirty-three of the inmates (52%) and twenty-seven of the wives (74%) whom we interviewed had participated in FRP for varying lengths of time.

The number of Family Reunion visits experienced by the inmates interviewed ranged from two to forty-eight, with a mean of 14.42 (SD = 12.65). Wives reported an average of 18.39 visits (SD = 17.81). The length of time over which the visits occurred ranged from about six months to several years. Fifty-eight percent of inmates and two-thirds of wives had participated in the program for at least two years. Thus, there was substantial variability among the group in how extensive and intensive their visits had been. In general, visits occurred at intervals of two to six months.

Because conjugal visits have been studied so little, not much has been written about what typically occurs during this type of extended family visit. Both inmates and wives were asked what they did on these visits. The popular stereotype seems to be that their primary function is sexual release for the couple (Burstein, 1977). The data suggest otherwise. The most common activity mentioned by 82% of the participants was talking. The majority (73%) also mentioned that they played games (up to three answers per inmate were coded, so percentages add to more than 100%). Over half (55%) also said that they cooked food and ate together, either inside the trailers or outside at picnic tables during nice weather. Thirty percent said that they watched TV. Only two (6%) mentioned sex, perhaps due to embarrassment. The presence of children in most cases may also have reduced opportunities for having sexual relations unless the children were asleep.

Virtually all of the inmates (97%) said they spend some time alone with their wives on a typical visit, and 84% reported spending time alone with their children.

It would appear that from the inmate's perspective, the activities composing a typical Family Reunion visit closely resemble family life during a weekend or vacation. Family members spend time together talking, playing, eating, and watching television. This makes sense insofar as it is exactly these aspects of family life that inmates reported sorely missing and that cannot be replicated inside the prison environment.

Wives

Wives' responses regarding what occurs during a typical Family Reunion visit are similar to those of their inmate husbands with two exceptions. The majority (73%) said that they talk, and 58% said they cook and eat together. Twenty-seven percent mentioned watching television and reading as a family. However, fewer (47%) mentioned playing with the children, and many more mentioned having sex (30%). All but two (93%) concurred with their husbands that they have the opportunity to spend time alone with their husbands, and 79% agreed that their husbands spend time alone with the children.

Again, the picture that emerges is one of a family engaging in activities together that are typical of family life: talking, playing, reading, watching TV, and eating meals. It is not surprising that fewer wives mentioned playing with the children, an activity that they presumably have many more opportunities to pursue than their husbands. However, it is somewhat unexpected that so many more wives than inmates would mention sexual relations, although this group still composes a minority of the sample.

IMPACT OF FAMILY REUNION VISITS

Inmates

In addition to wanting to know what Family Reunion visits were like, we were also interested in how the participating family members felt about these visits and accordingly we asked: "What is the perceived impact of FRP visits on inmates, wives, and children?"

The modal inmate response to the question "How do you feel about the visits?" was that they liked or loved them, an opinion held by 61% of those who had experienced FRP visits. Another 24% said that the visits helped them to spend time with and to feel a part of their families. Only one inmate held the more neutral view that the visits simply allowed him the opportunity to get out of his cell.

Virtually all of the inmates whose children participated in Family Reunion visits also felt that the children liked or loved the visits, with some noting that as the children got older they preferred not to come. This phenomenon may parallel the drop-off of interest in post-divorce child visitation to the homes of noncustodial parents that occurs once children become adolescents.

We were also interested in whether or not inmates perceived that their relationships with their wives and children had changed at all as a function of their participation in FRP visits. Eighty-two percent reported that their marital relationships had changed, in all cases for the better. Specifically, 59% said they felt closer to their wives as a result of the visits, and 37% said they felt better able to express themselves and communicate with their wives. Two said they felt more committed to the relationship due to the visits. A smaller but still substantial number (62%) reported that their relationships with their children had changed as a result of the visits.

Wives

Wives' perceptions about FRP visits were more varied than their husbands'. In terms of how they felt about the visits, the most common responses were "they are OK" and "they help the relationship," both views held by 28% of the sample. Twenty-one percent said they wished the visits could last longer or were more frequent. A few wives (7%) felt that they participated primarily for their husbands, who benefited more than they did. However, despite their more varied perceptions about the visits, 90% of those who participated felt that their relationship with their husband had changed as a result of the visits, primarily because they had gotten closer (59%) or they fought less (7%).

Regarding wives' perceptions of how their husbands' relationships with their children were affected by participation in FRP, three-quarters felt that the father-child relationship had improved, and one-quarter said it stayed the same. No one felt the father-child relationship had worsened as a result of such visits. Improvement took place because the children had an opportunity to get to know their fathers better than they would have if they had not been able to participate in these extended family visits, which take place in a more natural atmosphere than the traditional visiting room.

To conclude, Family Reunion visits occur relatively infrequently but are still seen by participants as a meaningful opportunity to simulate some aspects of a normal family life. Family members spend time talking, playing, cooking, eating, reading, and watching television together. Most inmates have the opportunity to spend some time alone with their wives and their children. Most family members who participate seem to enjoy the experience, although in some ways the visits appear to benefit inmates more than the wives or the children, especially the older children. Insofar as wives bear almost the total burden of preparation for the visits, which can be complicated and costly since they must bring all the food for the visit and travel long distances by bus, often with young children in tow, it is not surprising to learn that their enjoyment of the visits may be somewhat less than that of their husbands. These findings are consistent with those of a California study of inmates who received conjugal visits. Burstein (1977) reported that the wives who made conjugal, as opposed to traditional, visits were almost twice as likely to encounter serious practical and financial difficulties in making visits to their husbands.

FAMILY REUNION PARTICIPATION AND COPING

Another question of interest was whether or not the quality of coping was affected by the opportunity to experience conjugal visits. Thus, we asked: "Is participation in FRP associated with enhanced coping?" Table 6.1 depicts F-COPES scores for inmates and wives according to their participation in FRP or lack thereof. Comparisons with existing norms indicate that total coping scores are all above the fiftieth percentile and are highest for nonFRP wives, who are coping at the eightieth percentile. T-tests indicate that nonFRP wives are coping significantly better overall than are FRP wives [$t = 2.33$, $df = 34$, $p < .006$].

Examination of subscale scores reveals only one group difference related to FRP participation: There was a trend for nonFRP wives to score higher on Seeking Spiritual Support when compared to FRP wives [$t = 1.88$, $df = 30$, $p < .055$]. This trend suggests that wives who have not participated in FRP are more likely to turn to religion as a means of coping, compared to those who have had Family Reunion visits.

Overall, findings regarding coping among inmates and wives as a function of participation in FRP indicate an association between program participation and enhanced coping only for wives but not in the expected direction. This is primarily explained by the trend

Table 6.1
Mean F-COPES Scores for Inmates and Wives According to Family Reunion Participation

| | Family Reunion Program[1] | | | | | | Non Family Reunion Program[2] | | | | | |
| | Inmates | | | Wives | | | Inmates | | | Wives | | |
	M	SD	%	M	SD	%	M	SD	%	M	SD	%
Social support	24.06	7.35	35	25.55	7.12	37	25.11	8.23	40	25.45	6.56	37
Reframing	34.09	5.84	83	32.56	5.66	77	34.12	4.80	83	33.92	6.04	82
Spiritual support	14.12	4.83	26	16.23	3.99	40	16.67	3.50	66	17.60	2.12	73
Mobilizing for help	12.50	4.41	61	13.35	3.73	59	12.64	4.00	61	13.67	2.93	60
Passive appraisal	14.76	4.18	98	13.91	3.32	97	14.29	4.05	97	15.75	3.62	99
Total	99.42	16.64	71	97.29	24.01	55	100.54	11.13	73	105.25	10.30	81

[1] Ns range from thirty-two to thirty-three for inmates and twenty-two to twenty-four for wives.

[2] Ns range from twenty-six to twenty-eight for inmates and ten to twelve for wives.

toward nonFRP wives being more likely to seek out sources of spirituality as a means of coping, as compared to wives who had participated in FRP.

FAMILY REUNION PARTICIPATION AND FAMILY FUNCTIONING

Communication

It is possible that participation in FRP could have an impact on a variety of different measures of family functioning, and we posed a series of questions to explore this possibility. We asked first: "Are there differences in inmate-wife communication based on Family Reunion Program participation?"

Inmates. We examined frequency distributions on measures of communication as a function of FRP involvement of inmates. We discovered using chi-square analysis that there are no significant differences between FRP and non-FRP inmates on the following variables: frequency of seeing one's wife or writing her letters; perceived effects of phone calls on the relationship; frequency of talking to one's children by phone or writing to them.

However, there were some significant differences related to FRP participation. FRP inmates were significantly more likely than nonFRP inmates ($X^2 = 5.43$, $df = 1$, $p < .02$) to talk to their wives every two weeks or more often. Ninety-four percent of FRP inmates talked to their wives that frequently, in contrast to 57% of nonFRP inmates. In addition, there was a trend for nonFRP inmates to see their children more often than those in FRP ($X^2 = 3.18$, $df = 1$, $p < .07$). Forty-four percent of nonFRP inmates saw their children at least every two weeks, compared to 21% of FRP inmates. The remainder of both groups saw their children less frequently. Although more nonFRP inmates saw their wives weekly compared to those in FRP (32% versus 18%), this relationship did not achieve statistical significance.

Wives. The differences in communication reported by inmates were not reflected in wives' reports of their communication with inmates when FRP group comparisons were made. No significant group differences were obtained on frequency of telephone conversations, frequency of writing letters, or perceived impact of phone calls on the relationship. Thus, wife communication was found not to differ as a function of FRP participation. This may be explained by the fact that some wives of FRP inmates did not participate in the study.

Decision Making

We surmised that the opportunity to have more extended visits might affect the decision-making patterns employed by couples who participated in Family Reunion as compared with those who were limited to more traditional means of communication. We asked: "Are there differences in decision making based on FRP participation?"

We examined decision making at the time of the interview by looking at both the individual items and the overall decision-making scale (see Chapter 5) separately for husbands and wives. In looking at decision making in the aggregate, no FRP group differences emerged for either wife or inmate decision making. The mean scale scores for FRP and nonFRP wives were 24.20 (SD = 4.74) and 24.75 (SD = 3.55), respectively. The mean decision-making totals for husbands were 21.75 (SD = 3.55) for FRP inmates and 20.18 (SD = 3.26) for nonFRP inmates.

Because the total scores could mask differences in individual items, group differences were examined at that level. Among wives, one trend emerged on the item "Who decides about child discipline?" (X^2 = 5.24, df = 2, $p < .07$). In the nonFRP group, half of the wives said that decision making on this issue is more under their control, while the other half said both spouses have equal say. However, among FRP wives three-quarters said they decide on these matters, with 16% saying both spouses have equal say and the remaining 8% saying their husbands decide about child discipline. Thus, decision making on this issue appears to be somewhat more polarized according to FRP wives, although it might have been expected that FRP visits would promote more joint decision making.

Among inmates, two significant differences regarding decision making emerged. Again, on the child discipline question, there was a signficant difference related to FRP participation (X^2 = 8.90, df = 2, $p < .02$). According to husbands, decisions about child discipline were more dominated by the wife in the FRP group, where 88% said their wives made these decisions all or most of the time, in contrast to just over half of inmates (57%) in the nonFRP group. This closely parallels the reports of wives. A similar pattern emerged with respect to making decisions about how much to spend: FRP husbands reported signficantly greater wife influence than nonFRP husbands ($X^2 = 9.49$, $df = 2$, $p < .007$). Ninety-one percent of FRP inmates reported that their wives make these decisions all or most of the time, in comparison with 57% of nonFRP inmates reporting this pattern.

In summary, although FRP differences do not emerge when wife or husband decision making is examined overall, examination of individual items reveals differences on two items. Inmates and wives concurred that decisions about child discipline are more controlled by .the wife among those who have Family Reunion visits. In addition, while wives in both FRP and nonFRP groups agreed that they have disproportionate influence over how much is spent on various items, only FRP inmates reported such a pattern of decision making. Perhaps extended visits provide the inmate with more opportunity to see what his wife's life is like without him and the extent to which she must manage day-to-day decisions on her own. In contrast, wives who only have traditional, briefer visits may prefer to avoid difficult issues such as money management, allowing their husbands to maintain the illusion that they still have significant influence over these issues. Unfortunately, the incarceration and family life literature offers little insight into these findings.

Cohesion and Adaptability

We also speculated that differences in marital functioning might be associated with participation in FRP and asked, "Are couples who have participated in FRP more cohesive, more adaptable, and more satisfied with their marriages than those who have not participated?"

Husbands. Means and standard deviations on FACES III scores are depicted in Table 6.2. It can be seen that the means on cohesion, adaptability, and family satisfaction are quite similar, and *t*-tests indicate that there are no signficant differences on these measures as a function of FRP participation. Based on Olson et al.'s (1985) norms, both FRP and nonFRP inmates are on the line between the "separated" and "connected" categories on cohesion, and both fall into the "chaotic" range on adaptability.

Table 6.2
FACES III Scores According to Family Reunion Participation

	Inmates			Wives		
	n	M	SD	n	M	SD
Cohesion						
FRP	33	40.61	6.57	23	40.74	5.17
NonFRP	28	41.14	6.51	12	41.58	5.63
Adaptability						
FRP	33	32.61	7.33	25	31.04	8.12
NonFRP	26	31.65	5.86	12	32.92	7.40
Family satisfaction						
FRP	32	8.75	9.81	23	13.74	12.48
NonFRP	33	7.00	7.48	12	13.33	13.64

Wives. Findings for wives were parallel. The means shown in Table 6.2 are quite similar for FRP and nonFRP wives. Both groups of wives score at the border of the "separated" and "connected" ranges on cohesion. Like their husbands, both groups of wives also fall into the low end of the "chaotic" range on adaptability. Again, there were no significant group differences on the basis of FRP particiption.

Emotional Closeness

We were also interested in whether or not participation in Family Reunion was associated with a greater degree of emotional closeness between the inmate and his family. Accordingly, we asked: "Are inmates and their wives who have participated in Family Reunion closer to one another than those who have not participated?"

Inmates. We compared mean responses to the question "How close do you feel to your wife now?" by FRP group and found that

FRP inmates reported being signficantly closer to their wives than nonFRP inmates [$t = 1.55$, $df = 57$, $p < .009$]. The closeness means for FRP and non-FRP inmates were 6.48 and 5.62, respectively.

Regarding wife closeness to husband, however, no group differences were observed. The closeness scores for FRP and nonFRP wives were almost identical: 6.36 and 6.33, respectively. Thus, participating in Family Reunion visits was related to inmates' perceived closeness to wives but was not related to wives' sense of closeness to husbands.

We also explored the inmate's closeness to his children from both his own and his wife's perspective by asking: "Are inmates who have participated in the FRP closer to their children than those who have not participated?" The pattern of findings was identical to that found with inmate-wife closeness. Based on inmate perceptions there was a significant group difference such that FRP inmates reported higher closeness scores than nonFRP inmates [$t = 1.45$, $df = 56$, $p < .03$]. The mean closeness rating for FRP inmates was 6.48 and for nonFRP inmates was 5.76.

However, once again, FRP group membership was not related to wives' perceptions of their children's closeness to the inmate. When asked, "How close do your children feel to your husband?" the mean closeness rating for FRP wives was 6.32 and for nonFRP wives was 6.30, a nonsignificant difference.

Finally, we asked inmates and wives who had participated in FRP about their closeness to one another and about the inmate's closeness to children retrospectively (before they had participated in Family Reunion visits), as well as at the current time, and compared their responses over time. Some interesting differences emerged. Among inmates, the preFRP mean closeness to wife was 4.94 (SD = 2.02), compared to 6.48 (SD = 1.15) after participation in Family Reunion visits, a highly significant difference [$t = 5.41$, $df = 32$, $p < .0001$]. The same pattern was observed for wives. The mean on preFRP closeness was 5.04 (SD = 1.97), in contrast to 6.38 after participation in FRP, a significant difference [$t = 3.56$, $df = 23$, $p < .002$].

Inmates evaluated their closeness to their children similarly. Before involvement in FRP the mean closeness to children was 5.29 (SD = 2.31), whereas after having FRP visits it was 6.45 (SD = 1.31), again a highly significant difference [$t = 2.85$, $df = 30, p < .008$].

These findings suggest the possibility that participation in Family Reunion visits has an enhancing effect on perceptions of closeness to spouse and children. However, it is also possible that these ratings were influenced by social desirability, especially since inmates and wives knew that we were studying the FRP. In addition, both ratings were obtained (pre- and postFRP visits) at the same point in time, although the questions were asked at different points during the interview to try to minimize any halo effect. The fact that the closeness ratings were not significantly different when FRP and nonFRP inmates and wives were compared also raises questions about whether or not the program has an impact on perceived closeness among family members.

SUMMARY

Approximately half of the inmates and three-quarters of the wives we studied had participated in FRP for varying lengths of time ranging from several months to several years. FRP visits provided inmates, wives, and their children with the opportunity to interact as a family unit, if only for brief periods of time. Inmates reported that the visits provided them with the opportunity to communicate with family members and express themselves to their wives and children, bringing them closer together as a family. Wives' experiences were more variable, often perceived as benefiting their husbands more than themselves by providing inmates with relief from the unpleasantness of prison life and the opportunity to maintain their relationships with their children. Wives frequently commented that the burden to prepare for the visits rested more heavily on their shoulders in terms of finding transportation to the prison setting, as well as packing clothing and food.

Although we expected to observe differences in the functioning of participants in FRP as compared with inmates and wives who could not participate, for the most part these differences did not materialize.

In regard to coping behaviors, there were no differences either in total coping scores or on the individual subscales for inmates. However, nonFRP wives had signficantly higher total coping scores, largely attributable to Seeking Spiritual Support and Passive Appraisal. Although all four groups had coping scores that were above the 50th percentile, among FRP participants inmates coped more effectively than their wives, whereas the reverse pattern was evident in the nonFRP group.

Few differences were observed in family communication as a function of FRP participation. Although both groups of inmates communicated with their children about equally, FRP inmates talked to their wives by phone more often than did nonFRP inmates. On the other hand, there was a trend for nonFRP husbands to see their children more frequently than FRP participants.

Regarding decision making, there were no differences in the overall score for either inmates or wives based on FRP participation. However, there was a tendency for both inmates and wives in the FRP group to say that wives had greater control over decisions about child discipline than husbands, as compared to nonFRP participants. FRP and nonFRP inmates differed about the amount of influence they perceived themselves having with regard to how much money to spend on household purchases, with FRP husbands reporting significantly more wife influence than did nonFRP inmates. Perhaps extended visits enabled FRP inmates to be more realistic about the family roles their wives had to perform in their absence and thus they had fewer illusions about the scope of their own influence over family decisions.

No group differences were observed when using the FACES III measures to compare FRP and nonFRP inmates and wives. All four groups were on the line between the "separated" and "connected" categories on cohesion, and at the low end of the "chaotic" range on adaptability.

On perceived closeness to wives, however, FRP inmates reported that they were significantly closer than did nonFRP inmates. This was also true for reported closeness to children: FRP inmates perceived themselves to be significantly closer than did nonFRP inmates. However, no differences in perceived closeness to husbands were found for wives as a function of participation in FRP; both groups reported themselves to be extremely close (over six on a seven point scale). Nor were there differences in wives' reports of their husbands' closeness to children when those who had FRP visits were compared with those who did not.

Finally, highly significant differences were found among FRP participants, both inmates and wives, with regard to their perceptions of closeness to one another before experiencing FRP visits compared to after having visits. The same relationship was observed between preFRP and postFRP closeness to children: Inmates perceived themselves to be significantly closer to their children after FRP visits than before they began.

To conclude, participation in the FRP was not related to coping, marital cohesiveness or adaptability, or communication among family members. On the other hand, it appears that FRP inmates may be more realistic about the extent of their influence over at least some aspects of family decision making. Finally, having conjugal visits may have enhanced inmates' feelings of closeness to their wives and children.

Chapter 7

Policies, Programs, and Services

The purpose of this chapter is to provide information about policies, programs, and services that can benefit inmates and their families as they struggle to cope with the experience of incarceration. Before describing such policies, programs, and services, it would be useful to identify the needs of inmates and prison families as both individuals and as members of a couple or family system, as such needs emerge from our findings and from the literature on incarceration and family life.

As far back as the late 1950s it was recognized that the family played an important role in facilitating the transition from the correctional institution to the community (Zemans and Cavan, 1958). In addition, we have learned that the inmate's relationship with his family influences how he functions and copes with the experience of incarceration while he is in prison. Although many offenders come from dysfunctional families that may have played a significant role in contributing to their criminality and are unlikely to play a major role in their rehabilitation (Fox, 1981; Ingram and Swartzfager, 1973), by no means is this the case for all, or even most, inmates. Thus, in many cases marital and family relationships have the potential to be rehabilitative and should be not only preserved but also strengthened.

Enlightened correctional policy would first recognize the importance of inmate-family relationships and second, encourage the maintenance of a strong, healthy bond between the inmate and his family. To foster such a bond in turn requires that correctional systems acknowledge the needs of inmate families and do what they can, within reason, to assist families to adapt to the imprisonment of a member. Most states have no formal system to help families cope with the inevitable problems associated with incarceration of a member or to assist them to negotiate the myriad correctional regulations affecting inmates and their families.

NEEDS OF PRISON FAMILIES

Inmates

Despite the fact that male inmates have family-related needs, correctional systems are more likely to ignore or neglect these needs in programming for male inmates than is the case for female inmates (Thomas, 1981). Inmates have three basic needs in relation to their families. First, they need social support and frequent, meaningful communication with family members, including wives and children, parents, siblings, and other relatives. Although letters and phone calls are important, face-to-face contact in the form of regular visitation is the most significant type of communication for maintaining and strengthening family bonds. Ideally, this should include conjugal visits for married inmates as well as home furloughs, in addition to traditional visits. The importance of conjugal visits, especially for inmates, is validated by our findings as well as those of others (Burstein, 1977; Howser et al., 1983; Howser and MacDonald, 1982). Regular visitation is especially important for inmates with young children, who otherwise might not have the opportunity to develop meaningful relationships with their fathers, particularly if the father is incarcerated for longer than a year or two. Our data establish how important the father role is for most inmates. Related to this is the need to be placed in a facility that is as close to their homes as possible so that the costs and inconvenience of visiting can be minimized.

Second, inmates need educational programming focused on family life. Their receptivity to such programming is evident in the findings regarding the high investment of inmates in their roles as fathers and husbands. Such programs can assist inmates to better understand the needs of other family members as well as imparting improved communication, problem-solving and conflict-resolution skills. Most inmates will return to their families, and those with children intend to resume their parental roles on release (Thompson, 1984). That being the case, programs are needed within correctional facilities to assist inmate fathers to better understand their marital and parental roles and responsibilities, and most are quite receptive to such programming (Sack et al., 1976). A study of 115 incarcerated men, 84% of whom were parents, found that 80% were interested in learning enhanced parenting skills, despite having limited contact with children and long sentences (Hairston, 1990).

Third, inmates need ready access to counseling to address their needs as individuals as well as members of a couple or family system. More than three-quarters of the inmates studied here identified family-related concerns as a stressor. In addition, the sizable and growing proportion of inmates with substance abuse problems strongly indicates the need for counseling specifically focused on alcohol and drug dependencies. This will have implications for their ability to be successfully reintegrated into their families and to refrain from criminal behavior in the future. Inmates also need to learn to manage aggression, increase self-esteem, and more effectively resolve the problems of daily living in a correctional facility. In addition, couple and family therapy should be made available to assist in coping with the stressful and difficult issues that arise when a man is temporarily separated from his family. This is discussed in depth in Chapter 8.

Wives

Many (probably most) wives of inmates receive both practical and emotional support from their own extended families and those of their husbands, as our data show. However, our findings also indicate that many still have significant unmet needs that their families cannot or will not address.

First, wives need timely information about the criminal justice system in general and the facility in which their spouse is incarcerated in particular. The general lack of information about these issues has been referred to as an "information crisis" (Jorgensen et al., 1986). Wives need concrete information about (1) how the facility operates, (2) its rules and regulations regarding visiting, (3) relevant resources and services to which they are entitled, and, if relevant, (4) when and where their husband will be transferred (Weintraub, 1976). Too often, inmates are placed in or transferred to facilities without their wives' knowledge. This information should be conveyed simply and clearly, whether in a brochure or orally by a counselor. Given the proportion of Spanish-speaking inmates, official information from prison facilities should be bilingual.

Second, concrete services are needed by many wives, especially those who have lost the sole or primary family breadwinner when their husband was incarcerated. Oftentimes wives are forced into the labor market, accepting low-paying jobs as a result of limited education and inadequate skills. Others are forced onto the welfare rolls. Many have young children and could benefit from other concrete services such as day care, subsidized housing, and job training. The heavy reliance on extended family members for financial assistance and babysitting found among the wives we studied underscores the need for these kinds of services.

Third, wives need affordable, convenient transportation to and from prison facilities since many lack such transportation or the resources to purchase it. Several wives told us that the high cost of visits, both traditional and FRP, was a barrier that prevented them from visiting as frequently as they or their husbands would have liked.

Fourth, wives need counseling services to help them manage the initial crisis and ongoing emotional strain of coping with a spouse who is in prison. There is the need for crisis intervention and short-term counseling as well as long-term counseling, if necessary. Wives need to learn strategies to manage the stigma, anxiety, confusion, and depression that often result from the temporary loss of their husbands. In addition, many wives need assistance in managing relationships with extended family members and friends who may blame them for their husband's incarceration or pressure them to end the relationship. Many prison wives, those studied here as well as others, also need help in assuming the new role of single parent, which most women find extremely challenging under the best of circumstances. In this case the task is even more difficult because the "family must redefine itself in the absence of the incarcerated member in such a way as to still include him" (Weintraub, 1976, 29–30).

Children

First and foremost, children need to be told the truth about where their father is in order to cope with his absence and minimize adjustment difficulties such as the depression, anxiety, acting out, and school difficulties that are so often associated with a father's imprisonment. Deception, although understandable and often well intended, rarely is successful in hiding the father's whereabouts and only contributes to a child's confusion.

Children need ready access to their fathers through frequent phone calls and letters, regular traditional visits, and the more extensive, face-to-face contact that is possible through conjugal visits and home furlough programs. The frequent communication between children and their inmate fathers found in our data may account for the feelings of father-child closeness reported by both inmates and the children's mothers.

Finally, children, too, need access to family and personal counseling services in order to express their feelings about having a father in prison and learn to cope with feelings such as anger and sadness, as well as their mother's reaction, peer relationships, and other difficulties.

In summary, inmates and their families have a variety of needs related to the experience of incarceration. Inmates need support and regular communication with family members, programs focused on family life, and individual and family counseling to help them address the inevitable family-related problems associated with being in prison. Wives, although on the outside, also have needs associated with their husbands' incarceration. They need accurate information about the criminal justice system, concrete services, affordable transportation to the facility, and counseling. Finally, children of inmates have needs as well. They need to know the truth about where their father is and why, and to have regular access to him and the opportunity to work through their feelings about having a parent in prison through professional counseling services if necessary.

POLICY ISSUES

The literature on incarceration and family life and the findings of our study suggest a number of policy recommendations that, if adopted more widely by federal and state correctional programs, would enhance the quality of inmate-family relationships. Incorporation of such policies and programs by correctional systems in turn may reduce recidivism in the long run, based on what we know about the potentially rehabilitative role of the family in the lives of incarcerated men. All of these recommendations are consistent with the policy recommendations on families of adult offenders published in the *Proceedings of the First National Leadership Conference on Families of Adult Offenders* held in 1988 in Waynesboro, Virginia, and endorsed by conference participants.

First, it should be the stated policy of each correctional system to encourage family contact and strengthen family relationships. This recommendation was made in 1973 by the National Commission on Criminal Justice Standards and Goals, and yet, too often, from the perspective of the inmate and his family, family visiting appears to be tolerated at best, rather than encouraged (Schafer, 1977). Although it is not the fault of the correctional system that inmates often have dysfunctional relationships with family members, it is in the best interest of the community in the long run for the criminal justice system to directly address those relationships when possible. Chaiklin (1972) has stated that "certain problems are so salient that for correctional services to ignore them is to guarantee the offender's return to prison or some other institution. One of these is re-establishing contact with relatives when the offender has been isolated" (789). The recognition of the importance of family contact should extend to those in common-law relationships as well as legal marriages, especially if there are children involved.

One specific way to operationalize such a policy would be through the establishment of an office or department of family relations whose purpose would be to facilitate contact with families, provide marital and family counseling, make referrals to appropriate community agencies, and facilitate family problem solving (Jorgensen et al., 1986). There is both symbolic and practical value in centralizing family support activities in one office.

The benefits of adopting such a profamily policy have been stated. Two possible obstacles exist. Some may feel that a profamily stance "coddles" inmates who are in prison to be punished. They need to be persuaded that since most inmates will return to society—and rather quickly—encouragement of family contact and addressing family-related needs benefits society as much as it does the offender. The cost of establishing such an office is another potential obstacle. However, in the long run improved family relationships, which may deter future criminality, could make these expenditures cost effective.

Second, in states where there is more than one facility in which an inmate can be placed, efforts should be made to place the individual in the facility closest to his or her home community. This offers obvious advantages in terms of facilitating visitation by friends and family, particularly in states such as California, New York, and Texas that are geographically large and have significant numbers of incarcerated individuals. Holt and Miller (1972) have noted that the farther the visitors have to travel in order to visit, the less likely they will be to visit regularly, especially if the sentence is long. Their findings indicate deterioration in contact with significant others, especially wives, even within the first year of the sentence. By the fourth year, just over half of the married men were still receiving visits, and visitation by common-law wives was very unlikely by the second year (Holt and Miller, 1972).

However, with rapidly expanding prison populations and more constrained budgets, altering correctional policy so as to make assignments closer to home may be even harder to implement in the future. A major drawback is that the need to place inmates as close to home as possible may reduce flexibility on the part of correctional officials at a time when placement options are more and more constrained by overcrowding and tight budgets.

Third, visitation by family members should be viewed as an inmate's right, not a privilege. Human contact should be viewed in the same way as are food and water—a necessity rather than a reward for good behavior. In addition, a more expansive definition of "family" would permit visits by common-law wives who share the parenting role with the inmate but who are not necessarily married (Bush, 1990). Prison visiting schedules should be flexible and permit frequent visiting in the least restrictive environment possible. Inmate fathers should have the same rights in relation to their children as do inmate mothers and have access to the same types of services, such as parent education (Boudouris, 1985). One low-cost method for obtaining such services would be to seek outside groups or volunteers who would be willing to provide such services to inmates.

The major obstacle to acceptance of this position is the belief that because offenders are incarcerated to be punished, anything that is perceived as rewarding, such as visits or special programming, should be seen as a privilege and allocated contingent upon good behavior, rather than being viewed as a right. As mentioned previously, the best argument against such a position is that promotion of visitation is a means of keeping the inmate connected to the community to which he is likely to return.

Fourth, consideration should be given to extending home furloughs more broadly for the purpose of solidifying family relationships and to introducing extended family visiting at correctional facilities, including conjugal visits, in those states that do not have them. The research conducted in New York State (Howser and McDonald, 1982) strongly suggests that participation in such visits is associated with reduced recidivism, and thus is cost effective. Extended visits such as these would allow for parents and children to have more normalized contact with one another and for the father to partake in the usual activities of the parent role. Although some states permit furloughs for this reason, many others do not. This is a less expensive method than conjugal visits for encouraging family ties in a natural environment for those inmates who are near the end of their sentences or not viewed as threats to the community. Data from states that permit furloughs to encourage and maintain family contact could be used to persuade correctional policymakers that this is a rational policy that benefits the community and is associated with few problems. However, such a policy may be politically unacceptable irrespective of data showing that few inmates commit new crimes while out on furlough.

Finally, it should be standard policy for correctional systems to form close linkages with community agencies that serve the families of inmates as well as inmates themselves on release. This means that facility staff must be knowledgeable about such resources and prepared to make appropriate referrals to relevant community agencies.

The feasibility of implementing such a recommendation may be low in large states with sizeable prison populations due to the large number of agencies in many different locations that might be providing services to families during an inmate's incarceration and to the offender after he is released. Although facility staff can be trained to interface effectively with community-based agencies, make referrals, and so forth, whether or not close linkages can be established with large numbers of agencies in different locations remains a challenge. If linkages to community agencies could be shown to be cost effective via a demonstration project funded federally or through private foundations, for example, state correctional systems might be more easily persuaded to invest the resources in this way.

PROGRAMS AND SERVICES

It has been said that "the most important program for a sizeable portion of inmates would be a program aimed at their families. The family, as strongly linked as it is to parole success, should not be passed off to other social service professionals or to volunteers" (Jorgensen et al., 1986, 51). This section will describe the important elements of a comprehensive family services program for incarcerated males.

Several assumptions underlie such a program. The first is that male inmates are as deserving and in need of family services as are female inmates. The second assumption is that we should "value care provided by fathers as highly as care provided by mothers" (Bush, 1990, 19). The third assumption pertains to the timing within which family services are offered.

There are two points at which family involvement or engagement is important: when the inmate is first incarcerated, to solidify family relationships, encourage mutual understanding and support, and facilitate adaptation (Holt and Miller, 1972); and (2) during the prerelease period, to promote reintegration into the family system and larger community (Fenton, 1959; Holt and Miller, 1972; Kaslow, 1978). Reintegration of the inmate into the family after release will be more difficult if there has been no meaningful contact during incarceration (Hairston and Lockett, 1987). The objective of providing services early in the sentence is to identify inmates who potentially have dysfunctional or problematic family relationships so that preventive or interventive work can begin immediately to strengthen those relationships. If family ties are broken, the family cannot play a rehabilitative role. Furthermore, any potential rehabilitative role will be influenced by what has occurred in the family as a result of the incarceration and associated separation (Fox, 1981). Healthier family ties can promote inmate adjustment to prison, thereby reducing inmate management problems within the facility.

The final assumption of a comprehensive prison family services program is that it should include not only services provided within the facility but also linkage to appropriate agencies in the community. Described in the following sections are the critical elements of a family services program for inmates.

Services Within the Facility

Counseling. Several types of counseling services should be provided. First, individual counseling that is focused on the practical concerns of inmates rather than in-depth exploration of past issues or deep-seated mental health problems should be made available. While there is also a place for more in-depth psychotherapy for inmates with serious mental health problems, such services need not be provided within the context of a family services program. Instead, the focus should be on identification of family-related problems and helping the inmate to strengthen his support system on the outside (Showalter and Hunsinger, 1985).

In addition to individual counseling, marital or couples counseling should be available to assist both legally married and common-law couples address the difficulties of maintaining a relationship while the male partner is in prison. Attention should be devoted to issues such as (1) helping each partner to empathize with and understand the unique adjustment difficulties of the other, (2) discussing each partner's guilt or anger at the other due to the incarceration, (3) helping each to be supportive to the other in the interest of promoting enhanced coping with the incarceration experience, (4) promoting healthy communication, and (5) promoting joint decision making and problem solving regarding children, finances, relationships with extended family members, and so forth. Focusing on these issues will help each partner cope more effectively with the stress of the husband's incarceration, as the data illustrated. In addition, attention to these concerns should stabilize and strengthen the marital relationship, increasing the likelihood that it will survive the offender's imprisonment.

Fenton (1959) provides a detailed description of a model family counseling program employed in the California prison system. The family was broadly defined to include not only blood relatives but also friends and others with a serious interest in the inmate who would play a role in their lives during the incarceration period. Counseling was offered to families even before the inmate arrived at his destination facility, while he was still in the reception-guidance center. It was assumed that the shock of having a family member incarcerated and concerns about the future would serve as motivators to engage families in treatment, beginning with an orientation program about the facility. Family members were encouraged to think about how they may have played a contributing role in their loved one's criminal behavior and to think about how they might be helpful to the inmate, regardless of whether or not their actions encouraged his criminality.

During the orientation period, the idea of individual and group counseling either at the facility or in the community was introduced to family members. Four levels of family counseling services at the facility were defined: orientation and education regarding prison life; short-term individual and group casework focused on the inmate's experiences, such as what he was learning and the work he does; more in-depth psychotherapy designed to provide insight into the inmate's needs; and more intensive psychotherapy designed to lead to insights about whether or not (and how) the family member's behavior may have contributed to the inmate's criminality (Fenton, 1959).

Groupwork. Groups, both self-help and professionally led, are another needed service from which inmates and their families can benefit. Although not all inmates or family members are good candidates for groups, many are both appropriate for groups and receptive to the potential benefits of group membership. Groups offer their members the opportunity to pursue common goals while giving and receiving social support, achieving mutual understanding of common situations, acquiring new information, learning new skills, and giving and receiving assistance with problem solving. The fact that 82% of the inmates studied here identified family concerns as a major source of stress points to the potential usefulness of groups for addressing these concerns. Such groups could benefit not only married inmates but also those in common-law relationships and younger inmates who may be returning to their parents' homes.

Inmates can benefit from groups with a variety of different family-related foci, such as (1) the difficulty of maintaining a marriage while incarcerated, (2) the challenges of being a parent while incarcerated, and (3) coping with the end of a relationship while incarcerated.

Couturier and Cohen (1991) described one such group called the Incarcerated Fathers Group. Held at the State Correctional Institution in eastern Pennsylvania, the group meets every other week for one and a half to two hours. The purpose is to "provide participants with a supportive forum to share their experiences and frustrations with being 'long distance' fathers in prison, discuss special problems they encounter, and develop strategies to enrich and/or renew the family contact which they might have lost" (5). Issues that have been addressed include how to deal with your wife's anger that she must be a single parent because you are in prison, frustration over having so little input into your children's lives, and strategies for encouraging a reluctant child to communicate with you (Couturier and Cohen, 1991).

Family members of inmates, specifically wives, parents, and children, can also benefit from groups sponsored by the correctional institution. While many may not be interested in receiving formal therapy, they may be able to benefit from a group focused on how they can support and help the inmate and understand his experience. For example, ways of including the inmate in family decision making and problems relating to his extended family, concerns expressed by the wives studied here, could be usefully addressed in such a group. However, the distance factor can serve as a barrier to regular participation, especially in large states (this problem was experienced in the program described by Fenton [1957]).

Children, too, can benefit from the experience of participating in a group during a visit to the inmate. Such a group would give the inmate and his wife a chance to spend some time alone without having to worry about supervising the child during the visit, while allowing the child to interact with other children who also have an incarcerated father. If well-structured, such groups can provide children with an opportunity to share feelings of anger and embarrassment, while discussing their individual situations and gaining support.

Parent Education. The inmates whom we studied uniformly reported that the father role was very important to them and that they felt very close to their children. Others have found that the father role is not only important to new male inmates but may even become more important during the course of incarceration (Fox, 1981; Lanier, 1987; Sack et al., 1976). Collectively, these findings indicate that the father role is highly salient to most inmates who have children. Because most inmates will resume the father role on their release and many could benefit greatly from information about child development and parenting, a parent education program is a potentially valuable service. It has been observed that "we heard prisoners express the wish to be better parents when they go out. In fact, the parental role seemed to be the area in which they struggled most to see themselves positively. With other positive social roles denied them through incarceration, the importance of their role as parents grew" (Sack et al., 1976, 624). Parent programs can be particularly valuable in that many inmates do come from dysfunctional families where they have received inadequate parenting that may have, in part, contributed to their criminal behavior and that prepares them poorly for assumption of the parent role. Prison-based parent education programming should be sensitive to the ethnic distribution of the inmate population and avoid exclusive promotion of white, middle-class values. Community-based resources such as family and children's services agencies, child guidance clinics, or mental health centers may be useful in provision of parent education programming.

At least two such programs have been described in the literature. Marsh (1983) has described a small model program in Idaho that provided parent education to inmates and their wives. The focus was on child discipline, providing positive reinforcement, parent-child communication, and recognition of and response to children's feelings.

The Parents in Prison program described by Hairston and Lockett (1987) has a somewhat different orientation in that it is run by the Tennessee inmates whom it serves. It, too, aims to provide child development information and enhanced communication skills, but it also addresses the impact of incarceration on the family from the inmate's perspective and aims at improved inmate-family relationships in general. It employs classroom, experiential, and home-study components as well as monthly special events such as speakers on family-related topics and special projects that emphasize "family cohesion and support and the prevention of child abuse and neglect" (Hairston and Lockett, 1987, 113). Whereas parts of it are geared toward specific subgroups of inmates, other components are addressed to the entire inmate population.

Visitation Enhancement Programs and Services. Another component of a comprehensive family services program pertains to visitation and the ways in which correctional facilities can make the experience more pleasant for the inmate as well as his family. To a great extent this implies a new way of thinking about visitation, beginning with how visitors are treated when they first arrive at a facility (Fenton, 1959). Oftentimes the first visit is critical in forming attitudes about the facility and visiting in general (Fishman, 1981).

Much can be done to make visitation more satisfying and less artificial while respecting the need for security and concerns about contraband. Just the appearance of the visiting room can be an indication of how visitation is regarded within a particular correctional system. Whereas some visiting rooms are institutional in appearance, depressing, or even dirty, other rooms are cheerful and inviting, conveying the idea that visitation is viewed as valuable and important.

A national survey of state correctional facilities regarding their policies on family communication revealed that while few of the forty-four responding jurisdictions had policies specifically governing parent-child communication, all had policies regulating contact between inmates and family members. Individual facilities were found to have great discretion regarding frequency, length, times, and days of visitation. Eighteen states had policies regulating children in the visiting room, with the focus on the adult's responsibility to control children's behavior (Hairston and Hess, 1986). The authors concluded that "the restrictions placed on social interactions between parents and children during visits and the focus on discipline and control of children without provision of child-centered activities further serve as barriers to the strengthening and maintenance of parent-child attachments" (32).

However, a positive new trend in many facilities is the creation of children's centers where there are games and toys, organized activities, and in some cases child care provided by trained inmates or volunteers. These areas for children can consist of special rooms or just a corner of the general visiting room. When the weather is warm enough to be outside, special areas for children may be set aside outdoors. This trend recognizes that children have special needs during a lengthy visit. In addition, providing a special, supervised area for children can make the visiting room more orderly and give adults privacy and the opportunity to discuss sensitive issues without children overhearing.

One way to make visiting an enjoyable experience is by sponsoring a number of special events throughout the year celebrating various different holidays and events, such as Mother's Day, Father's Day, and Black History Month. For example, Lanier (1989) described the first Father's Day held at Eastern Correctional Facility in Napanoch, New York. Inmates themselves planned the day's events, which were designed to resemble a family picnic, including music, badminton, and ice cream cones for dessert.

Schneller (1990) has suggested that visitation should be used more systematically to have facility-sponsored Family Leisure Activities that are designed to help inmates and their families more closely approximate a normal family life. Examples of such activities include attendance at religious services together, sharing meals together, participating in both passive (i.e., TV) and active (i.e., volleyball) recreational activities, and marital activities, such as having discussions about the children or extended family relations. Such activities may be as useful as more traditional counseling services like couples therapy, and are likely to attract a broader group of inmates (Schneller, 1990).

In summary, a variety of facility-based family services have been described as components of a comprehensive family services program for male inmates. These include individual, couple, and group counseling; self-help groups for inmates as well as family members; parent education programming; and services and activities in conjunction with visitation by family members.

Community-Based Family Services

In addition to offering prison-based services to inmates and their families, correctional systems need to forge links with community agencies that (1) work with families in the community and/or (2) are willing to work cooperatively with prison officials to provide family-related services within the facility (Thomas, 1981). This type of linkage has become increasingly important as correctional budgets swell to accommodate ever increasing numbers of inmates, often leading to cutbacks in rehabilitative services offered by the correctional system. To accomplish this, correctional staffs will need to be knowledgeable about resources within the community that are of potential benefit to inmates or their loved ones.

A family's success in playing a rehabilitative role vis-à-vis the inmate will be related to its internal resources, as discussed at length in Chapter 2. However, a family's external resources, such as economic support, friends, and extended family, are also important. Socially isolated families will be much less effective at providing support to the inmate (Fox, 1981). In addition, inmates with strong family ties are likely to be more motivated to find and keep a job upon release, because employment will enhance their standing within the family (Fox, 1981). Thus, how well an inmate's family functions on the outside will indirectly affect how the inmate functions within the facility. The high percentage of inmates identifying stress associated with family concerns in our study underscores this need. In this sense, it is in the best interest of correctional staff to help families find the services they need to function optimally in their home communities. In addition, since most inmates will return to their communities relatively quickly, it is also in the community's best interest to play an active role in providing services on behalf of inmates (Fenlon, 1972).

Prerelease programs are a good example of a type of service where linkage with the community is essential (Chaiklin, 1972). Given what being released to the community represents for most offenders and their families, it is important to prepare all involved for what they can expect to encounter. Much of what is being done to prepare inmates for release is focused on securing employment, with family issues receiving less attention. And yet, how the inmate adjusts to family life is likely to be a predictor of his general postprison adjustment (Kaslow, 1978).

Typically, families react to the imminent release of a loved one somewhat ambivalently. While there is relief and joy that he will soon be coming home, there is also likely to be apprehension about what his return will mean to the family and whether or not he will be able to refrain from criminal activity (Kaslow, 1978). To prepare inmates and their families for release, a number of services can be used. First, prerelease meetings for families can be sponsored by the facility in conjunction with a visit. Many of the issues are sufficiently generic that they need not be discussed initially on an individual basis.

Eventually, it is advisable to have counseling, individual or couple, available to ease the transition back to the family and community. Oftentimes, the man who is released is a very different person from the one who entered the facility one or more years ago. He can be more self-aware, more mature, more educated, and free of the drug or alcohol dependency with which he may have entered the system; or, conversely, he can be more hardened and convinced he can "beat the system," ready to return to a life of crime. Ideally, those working on prerelease counseling within facilities should meet with those community-based counselors who are working with their families (Fenton, 1959).

Some of the issues that should be addressed in pre- and postrelease counseling include (1) feelings about what life was like during incarceration and expectations about what life will be like when the inmate is home; (2) how the ex-offender will fit into the family constellation that has evolved during his absence, including what roles he will perform and who might be displaced by his return; and (3) how the children are feeling about their father's reentry into the family (Kaslow, 1978). Thus, the issues that must be addressed in counseling about release pertain to feelings, relationships, and roles (family, work, and criminal).

Other services to families of inmates are best offered within the community. Such services must be provided by paid or volunteer staff who are knowledgeable about and sympathetic to the issues and strains associated with having a family member who is incarcerated. Numerous examples of such programs can be found in the literature, a few of which are described here.

A critically important service that community agencies can sponsor is self-help groups for wives and groups for children who have an incarcerated parent. The difficulties of prisoners' wives have been well documented in earlier chapters. Having a structured opportunity to get together with other wives in similar circumstances can be invaluable as a way of validating their emotional responses to their experiences, gaining needed social support, and sharing information about the correctional system. Crosthwaite (1972) described one such group in London, part of a national network of groups led by volunteers all over England.

A model program called Women in Crisis is offered to women with a loved one in prison in Connecticut. Relying heavily on trained volunteers, the program is organized around four different crisis points related to the stages of imprisonment: presentencing; sentencing day itself; initial incarceration; and pre- and postrelease. Volunteers help women with both practical (for example, finding a new apartment or arranging child care, two concerns expressed by the wives in this study) and emotional concerns (for example, providing support on sentencing day, accompanying someone on their first prison visit, or providing assistance with reestablishing ties to estranged children). Volunteers are also available to serve as advocates for the women if that is necessary.

Several other examples of programs aimed at providing social support and other services to wives of inmates deserve mention. An innovative project in Florida has provided services to wives of federal prisoners in a maximum security facility in Tallahassee, many of whom must travel a great distance to maintain contact with their husbands. The goal of the Family Living Project was to develop a site where wives could obtain affordable lodging, food, transportation to the facility, and child care in order to maximize the visitation experience. Additional objectives were to provide information and other resources to wives and to encourage their participation in groups focused on gaining support from other prison wives, problem solving, coping with the early stages of incarceration, and coping with the reintegration of their husbands into the family. The project began as an extension of a program providing group counseling to inmates with the goal of improved family relationships. In the course of offering the group it was discovered that many wives could not visit regularly because of the distance and associated problems, difficulties expressed by the wives we studied as well. Like the Women in Crisis program previously described, the Family Living Project relied heavily on trained volunteers, as well as social work students (Fenlon, 1972; Ingram and Swartzfager, 1973).

A similar program has been described in Britain, where a hostel was created to accomodate five families of prisoners during visits to the correctional facility. Over time, a self-help function evolved that assisted the families in coping with their fear, isolation, and stigma in response to the experience of incarceration (Horton and Wright, 1976).

In California, Friends Outside, the largest organization nationally dedicated to helping prisoners' families, enjoys support by prison officials as well as inmates and their loved ones. Eighteen chapters, sixty-five paid staff, and 1,500 volunteers provide services that include family counseling and support, therapy to inmates, educational assistance to children of offenders, assistance with transportation to and from facilities, and advocacy. Help with transportation is especially important because so many inmates who come from southern California are housed in facilities in northern California (Kiersh, 1979). This problem parallels the situation in New York State, where most inmates come from the New York metropolitan area but are housed in facilities in upstate New York; the women in our sample noted the difficulty and cost involved in obtaining transportation to the facilities where their husbands were incarcerated.

Another community-based program geared toward families of offenders was described by Scott (1983). Similar to the Women in Crisis program, service delivery is organized around four stages in the incarceration process. During the pretrial period, outreach is used to identify families who have had a loved one arrested, to offer them support and information about the criminal justice system; the staff meets with children and helps the family get connected to social agencies if appropriate. Establishing a relationship with the family helps the team support them through the difficult period of the trial. If the offender becomes incarcerated, regular counseling with the wife and children may be necessary to assist them in coping with this crisis. This includes both practical assistance and emotional support, needs identified by the wives in our sample as well. During the prerelease period counseling resumes to help the family prepare for the inmate's return home. Ideally, counseling should continue after he has actually arrived home as well.

To summarize, in addition to facility-based services, community-sponsored services for the families of offenders are also necessary. One type of service helps to prepare the inmate and his family for release and reintegration into the family and community after a period of incarceration. Prerelease services can be offered at the facility, within the community, or at both levels. Other services to families are more efficiently or effectively offered in the community, especially those that benefit wives, children, and parents of men who are incarcerated. Such services are designed to help family members understand the criminal justice system as it affects their loved one, cope with the experience of having a significant other in prison, obtain needed services, and receive social support.

Chapter 8

Clinical Intervention with Inmates and Their Families

ORGANIZATIONAL ISSUES RELEVANT TO COUNSELORS

In a correctional facility, the effective counselor must be able to understand and function in a complex, bureaucratic, security-conscious organization. The counselor must also be able to consult with an interdisciplinary staff and relate to a varied inmate population. In the course of performing assessments and interventions on behalf of inmates, the correctional counselor must not only attend to inmates' personal and family needs but also take into account concerns about safety, complex staffing patterns that exert their own pressures and demands, and the limitations of the facility's programs. That is, evaluation and treatment plans are affected by the total prison environment, which positively or negatively influences the behavior of both inmates and staff. Thus, an ecological perspective for understanding human behavior is recommended, in which assessment and treatment are viewed within the context of the individual, his family, the facility, and the larger society.

This chapter addresses the organizational context for evaluation and treatment of male inmates and their families, the counselor's role within the correctional facility, and the different intervention strategies. Case examples are provided to illustrate effective treatment in prisons.

Inmates usually have multiple problems that require a range of different services and intervention strategies (Netherland, 1987). An understanding of the multidimensional difficulties existing for inmates and their families suggests that no one program, community agency, or facility can meet all their clinical needs. Traditionally, correctional counselors and caseworkers have striven toward the broad goal of inmate rehabilitation. However, optimism regarding the prospects of rehabilitating inmates has waned, and rehabilitation has become a more controversial goal.

Assisting inmates to adjust to prison life, strengthen or maintain healthy family ties, and learn how to refrain from future criminal behavior requires several attributes on the part of the counselor. These include: (1) an understanding of the sources of criminal behavior, (2) strong clinical intervention skills, (3) knowledge of resources within the facility and in the community, (4) the ability to work effectively in an interdisciplinary context, (5) knowledge of cultural diversity, and (6) self-awareness. These attributes are elaborated in the following paragraphs.

First, on a cognitive level, counselors need to recognize that the sources of criminality are complex and multifaceted and reside not only within the individual but also in the environment of which he is a product (Handler, 1975; Roberts, 1983). An ecological perspective is most useful here.

Second, correctional counselors and caseworkers need a variety of different assessment and intervention skills. Inmates have often experienced a great many developmental and social deprivations that impair their ability to maintain internal controls and achieve minimal social conformity. In addition, inmates and their families typically are experiencing a variety of psychosocial stressors concurrent with incarceration, as discussed in Chapter 2. These conditions present serious challenges to the correctional counselor or caseworker, necessitating solid clinical training. Being able to work with groups, families, and individuals, as well as having crisis intervention skills, are basic requirements to working in a prison facility. In addition, if the overarching goal of correctional counseling is to successfully integrate or reintegrate the offender into community life and family life, then the counselor must be an "advocate, educator, consultant, broker, planner, data manager, resource mobilizer, clinical behavior-changer, and liaison person" as well as a clinician in the narrow sense (Gaudin, 1984, 281; Roberts, 1983). Among other things, roles such as advocate, planner, and data manager are essential to bring about changes in policies that affect inmates' well-being.

Third, counselors need knowledge of resources, both within the facility and in the larger community, insofar as lack of access to or knowledge of resources can create or exacerbate inmate difficulties in the social, health, family, or psychological arenas (Handler, 1975).

Fourth, the ability to forge relationships with allied professionals within the facility and in community-based programs is a prerequisite for provision of good inmate and family care (Selsky, 1962; Weintraub, 1976). Large caseloads, bulging inmate populations, and restrictive budgets influence the ability of both staff members and inmates to cope with the prison environment (Gaudin, 1984). Oftentimes, the counselor must simultaneously juggle numerous institutional demands, inmate and family needs, and professional issues. In order to be effective, the counselor must advocate and serve as a broker with the administration and other personnel on behalf of inmates and their family members. Thus, the counselor must build linkages to other facility personnel and community programs.

Establishment of trustful working relationships with key staff persons and community agency representatives increases the likelihood of eliciting assistance from them on behalf of inmate clients (Jorgensen et al., 1986; Roberts, 1983). Reaching out to the chaplain, security staff, teachers, or other mental health staff, for example, leads to their input into the helping process while increasing the counselor's legitimacy within the institution (Gaudin, 1984). Developing networks within the facility and in the community also builds teamwork and helps to insure that all relevant professionals are kept informed about the inmate's progress. As Fenton (1959) pointed out, the treatment of the family unit of "adult offenders becomes possible when caseworkers in the communities who are dealing with the families and those in the prison who are responsible for the inmates work together" (123). Additionally, when community agencies, prison counselors, and other correctional staff work together toward the common goals of inmate and family stability and adaptability, family coping, and communication may improve. Sharing the clinical burdens among the facility's staff and community workers may also reduce counselor burnout.

At the same time, the correctional counselor is an agent of social control, employed in a setting where danger is pervasive and safety concerns must be paramount. Thus, the counselor may experience conflicting loyalties leading to questions such as, Who is the client—the inmate, a family member, the correctional officer, or the prison superintendent? (Roberts, 1983).

Fifth, since many prison populations are composed disproportionately of individuals from minority groups (Jamieson and Flanagan, 1989; Netherland, 1987; Showalter and Hunsinger, 1985), the counselor must also have an in-depth knowledge of normative cultural variations and the inherent strengths brought to the treatment process by inmates and family members from diverse cultural groups (Showalter and Hunsinger, 1985). In any one facility, members of the African-American, West Indian, Hispanic, Asian, and Native American cultures may be represented alongside white inmates. This cultural diversity can create tension among these groups as they vie for informal control of inmates' lives and resources within the facility. Being knowledgeable about the different religious, cultural, and familial traditions of these varied groups will aid the counselor in forming relationships with inmates and their families (Showalter and Hunsinger, 1985).

Finally, counselors must be aware of their own biases, prejudices, and sensitivities, not only about racial and ethnic mores but also about various family living alternatives, sexuality in prison, HIV infection, and other human conditions that the inmate and the family might bring to the treatment process. The counselor must also understand that he or she may be closely scrutinized or viewed with hostility by inmates and other staff persons. The white worker, in particular, must expect to be viewed with distrust by some nonwhite inmates and to be seen as being part of an oppressive society. Depending on the specific situation and personal style, the counselor may choose to respond by acknowledging differences, being empathic toward inmate concerns, and/or frankly confronting the issues through direct communication with the inmate. The ability to build trust with inmates and other staff persons is of prime importance in being an active, competent, and compassionate counselor (Fishman and Alissi, 1979).

Minority counselors, too, may experience difficulties in confronting issues of ethnicity. Some may feel an inappropriate level of responsibility for resolving racial tensions in the facility. Others may overidentify with or, at the other extreme, distance themselves from inmates and families of their own race or ethnicity (Solomon, 1979). The minority counselor must be cognizant of his or her professional needs and desires as well as race-related administrative and organizational tensions. Being aware of and confronting the inconsistencies will help in reducing the minority counselor's stress and potential for burnout.

CLINICAL TREATMENT ISSUES

Assessment

In the first phase of the helping process, the counselor must be able to evaluate the inmate and his family in context. This will necessitate systematic assessment of numerous aspects of the inmate's circumstances. Prior to intervening with the inmate and his family, several important clinical questions must be addressed. First, what are the circumstances that led to this incarceration? Is this the first time the offender has been in prison? What is the offender's motivation to obtain counseling at this time? What is his developmental stage? What strengths and liabilities do the inmate, his wife, and his family bring with them to the counseling process? What are his family circumstances? Is he legally married or in a common-law relationship? Are there discrepancies in how the relationship is described by him and his partner? Does he have children? If so, how many are there, and what are their ages? Is this a stepfamily? What kind of relationships does the inmate have with his spouse, children, and members of the extended family? Has the family been supportive in the past?

Irrespective of the type of family relationships the inmate had prior to incarceration, future relationships will be influenced by a variety of factors. One of the most important is the type of visitation that is possible, since visitation is a primary vehicle through which significant relationships are maintained. This in turn will be influenced by the facility's policies on visitation and whether or not there are any restrictions on an inmate's visitors as a result of the type of crime he committed or his institutional adjustment record. The facility's level of security may also dictate the extent of visitation possible, for example whether or not physical contact is permitted. Other factors will also be important, especially the distance of the facility from the inmate's family and significant others. Of particular interest to the inmate will be whether or not conjugal visits are available, and if so what is required to qualify for such visits.

Careful assessment of the quality of the inmate's family relationships is necessary. As noted earlier, many inmates do not have close, healthy family relationships at the time of incarceration, and over time these fragile relationships may deteriorate even further. If the family is to play a role in helping to prepare the inmate for return to the community, these relationships must be durable. Good relationships will need to be maintained and nurtured, and poor relationships will need to be repaired, if possible.

A good starting place is to examine the quality of family ties at the time of arrest. Most inmates are concerned with maintaining family relationships, and this may be used as a source of leverage to overcome resistance to treatment (Showalter and Jones, 1980). How did family members respond to the arrest, trial, and sentencing? Are there long-standing family issues, such as domestic violence or substance abuse, that have direct or indirect implications for how the family will react to this new stressor? How is the family reacting now to the inmate's incarceration? What does this separation mean for them on a day-to-day basis? Is there anger, sadness, relief, or a combination of feelings about the incarceration on the part of the inmate and the family (Cobean and Power, 1978)? Is the inmate aware of the impact of his incarceration on his significant others and is he empathic toward those on the outside? If not, can he be helped to become more sensitive to its impact on his loved ones? Is the family receptive to meeting with a facility counselor to discuss the inmate and his concerns at this time? If not, would they be receptive to a referral to a helping agency in their own community? If so, perhaps the facility counselor who is working with the inmate could interface with a community-based counselor working with the family as both sides work toward strengthening family ties (Rieger, 1973).

Intervention

A useful way of thinking about interventions on behalf of inmates and their families is according to the stages of the criminal justice process: from arrest, to trial, to initial entry into the prison system, incarceration, and to prerelease. At each stage of the process, a crisis may occur and specific clinical strategies may provide the means of helping inmates and their family members with coping and adaptation. It is helpful for prison counselors to remember that by the time a man has been incarcerated he and his significant others have already been through a great deal as a result of the arrest, trial, and conviction.

Generally, the counselor at all stages of the process is providing information to the family, using the therapeutic relationship as a vehicle to provide assistance, and using networking, referral, and advocacy as means for obtaining needed concrete services for the family, if appropriate (Fishman and Alissi, 1979). Using a social work paradigm as a model for intervention, Netherland (1987) stated:

The general casework and groupwork skills taught to social workers can be appropriately applied in working with correctional clients. Giving feedback, clarifying, questioning, summarizing, confronting, resolving conflicts, interpreting, intervening in crises, referring, formulating goals, interviewing, setting limits, and predicting behavior are all useful [skills] in working with correctional clients (356–357).

By the time of sentencing the family should begin to be aware that there will be an enforced separation imposed on them. Knowing that there will be a lengthy period of separation will create stress and tension for the offender as well as his family (Showalter and Jones, 1980). As a result, they will need information about the length of the sentence, where the inmate will be incarcerated, and the rules and regulations governing visitation and communication with the inmate.

In the initial stages of imprisonment both the inmate and the family need to learn how to deal with the grief reaction engendered by the arrest, trial, and sentencing. Most family members and inmates will experience serious loss as a result of their separation from one another. Helping family members to grieve this loss, get in touch with both their sorrow and their anger at the inmate and the society, and become self-sufficient and stable are important counselor tasks (Cobean and Power, 1978). Using resources in the community and extended family may aid the counselor in helping the family with their initial adjustment to the separation when they may have financial, housing, educational, employment, and emotional needs (Cobean and Power, 1978).

The conditions characteristic of many of our nation's prisons are appalling, with over half the states under court order to remediate conditions that have been ruled "cruel and inhuman." When these conditions are combined with an environment of intimidation and victimization, brutal sexuality, racial tension, daily regimentation, limited choices, and limited opportunities for contact with significant others, a major adjustment challenge is presented to the new inmate (Netherland, 1987). However, even within this difficult environment, there are choices and alternatives.

Inmates at the early stages of incarceration are often angry at the world as a result of having lost their freedom, family, and friends and being forced to live in the prison environment. Many disavow responsibility for their problems and instead blame others (Cobean and Power, 1978; Netherland, 1987; Showalter and Hunsinger, 1985). Family members may need assistance in understanding their loved one's reactive behavior and the facility's responses to it (Cobean and Power, 1978). Some inmates are bitter and use negative coping strategies such as fighting and arguing as a defense against their feelings of frustration and loneliness. Other inmates may become overtly depressed and suicidal (Cobean and Power, 1978; Showalter and Hunsinger, 1985). Appropriate institutional limit setting for behaviors that are destructive to the self and to others and other appropriate therapeutic interventions, including medication, may be needed. An important clinical task at this stage is to help inmates to understand and take responsiblity for their own behaviors and problems. This can be followed up with assistance in modifying dysfunctional behaviors in the hopes of promoting healthier adjustment to prison life (Netherland, 1987).

Most inmates value contacts with family and friends, and these relationships may be useful as a source of leverage to motivate inmates into therapeutic involvement (Showalter and Jones, 1980). Since family members are often acutely aware of the need for behavioral change on the part of the inmate, their involvement in counseling can stimulate or reinforce motivation for inmate participation. Issues such as the inmate's use of drugs or alcohol and dysfunctional behaviors may influence visitation privileges and, therefore, are relevant concerns for family members and appropriate targets for intervention. Where home furloughs and conjugal visits are possible, concomitant family or marital counseling should be strongly encouraged (Rieger, 1973).

Couple or family counseling may prove to be helpful for both the inmate and the family (Kaslow, 1978). Sessions can be scheduled in conjunction with regular visits or overnight stays. The most effective interventions are likely to be those that are reality-based, practical, here-and-now approaches to family work. Behavioral-communication approaches such as structural family therapy or family therapy based on multiproblem family treatment should prove to be the most useful types of interventions. Such approaches should be helpful in reducing inmates' resistance to therapy by including the family and they have been demonstrated to be useful tools in bringing about actual changes in inmate behavior and attitudes (Showalter and Jones, 1980; Kaslow, 1978).

Family ReEntry, a relatively new program in Connecticut, illustrates how family therapy can be used to assist offenders reentering the community and their families to reduce future criminality. Closely supervised volunteer counselors meet with offenders and family members using the intergenerational theories of Boszormenyi-Nagy and Spark (1973), the structural theories of Minuchin (1974), and the brief strategic approach of Erickson (Haley, 1973). The focus is on what has worked successfully in the past and the development of reality-based, present-oriented solutions to the problems associated with being released. Family sessions are employed in addition to weekly support groups and parenting workshops. Compared with inmates who have not participated in the program, those who received Family ReEntry services were less likely to escape while still incarcerated or to be rearrested one year later, despite not being entirely voluntary participants (Reed and Thornton, no date).[1]

Several generic goals are appropriate for most couples experiencing a husband's incarceration. These include:

1. helping the couple maintain their relationship or come to a mutually agreeable decision to end it;
2. learning effective communication skills;
3. becoming involved on a deeper affective level;
4. exploring family members' feelings and thoughts about the incarceration;

5. coming to terms with being an absentee parent and deciding how to tell the children about their father's situation;

6. helping children and parents to maintain a relationship with one another during incarceration;

7. disciplining the children;

8. coping with feelings of separation from one another, especially after visits;

9. helping the wife learn how to survive without the inmate;

10. discussing expectations, support, demands, and the lack of follow-through by the extended family;

11. exploring concerns about homosexuality, infidelity, AIDS, and the meaning of other relationships with other people;

12. exploring the use of community resources and the reasons for not using them;

13. discussing the attraction to criminal behavior and street living;

14. discussing how the family is changing and what new roles have emerged for family members at home;

15. learning how to anticipate consequences and avoid impulsive behavior;

16. preparing for parole hearings and their outcomes;

17. planning for a future life outside prison, and discussing how the new roles within the household may have displaced the absent parent and spouse;

18. planning to ease the inmate back into the work world, the family, and the community; and

19. learning how to deal with the possible ambivalence about release from prison and being reintegrated into the family and community (Kaslow, 1978; Showalter and Jones, 1980).

For those inmates whose partner cannot or will not participate in ongoing sessions with the prison counselor, coordination with community agencies may prove to be a useful adjunct to facility services. In fact, the inmate can be involved in one-partner "marital therapy" if his spouse cannot be involved (Freedman and Rice, 1977). Helping the inmate to honestly examine his feelings; confront his lack of genuine empathy towards his loved ones; learn how to cope with a divorce or not being home for a holiday, death, or other special family occasions; and come to terms with not being a day-to-day parent to a child may be accomplished therapeutically in the context of one-person marital therapy (Freedman and Rice, 1977). Additionally, helping the inmate to use furloughs, conjugal visits, letter writing, and phone contacts productively can be helpful in promoting family cohesion and adaptability.

EXAMPLES OF CLINICAL INTERVENTIONS

The following case illustrations are offered to demonstrate some of the ways in which clinical interventions can be used to assist inmates with family-related problems. They are based on composites of inmates studied for the project.

Case Number 1: Julio Rodriguez and Maria Alvarez

Julio Rodriguez, age twenty-nine, has a twenty-three-year-old common-law wife, Maria Alvarez, who is six months pregnant. They already have two other children, Rosa, age seven, and Martin, a developmentally delayed three-year-old. They have been living together off and on for seven years, residing in various public housing projects. Julio has intermittently held unskilled, blue-collar jobs, and Maria receives Public Assistance for herself and her two children. Maria grew up in the same neighborhood as Julio, and they met through Maria's older brother who served some time with Julio in a detention center for delinquent youth.

Julio has been sentenced to prison for a second time for robbery and assault, as well as possession of an illegal firearm and a controlled substance. He has served five months of a seven to ten year sentence. The prison, Upper River Correctional Facility, is located 250 miles from where Maria and the children live. Just prior to Julio's incarceration, the county welfare department assisted Maria in finding afterschool day care for Rosa and a special preschool program for Martin. Maria has been receiving counseling from a local mental health clinic that specializes in services to Spanish-speaking clients. After the baby's birth, Maria wishes to return to school for vocational training and to receive her general education diploma.

The prison's counselor became aware of Julio's situation during the family's first visit to the facility, when Rosa clung to Maria. The counselor assigned to the visiting room that Saturday noticed that Rosa had temper tantrums and outbursts of crying during the visit. While attempting to assist Julio with Rosa, Maria blurted out in Spanish that she was never returning to visit her husband. Julio slapped Maria in response. As a result, he was detained by a correctional officer.

The counselor on duty knew some Spanish and brought Maria and Rosa to his office. Rosa played on the floor with some toys while the counselor and Maria talked about her living situation. Through crisis intervention techniques, ventilation, clarification, and focusing in on Maria's feelings, the counselor learned that Maria was ambivalent about the relationship. Her parents were pressuring her to stay away from Julio, and she was tired of living a life of loneliness, uncertainty, and poverty. She wanted more for herself and the children. Maria reported that she was tired of Julio's criminal behavior, and getting to the prison facility to visit was a real hardship. Ignorant of a community agency's transportation assistance program, Maria had relied on public transportation. Maria told her daughter that they were going to visit her father in the country, without really explaining the circumstances. She avoided telling Rosa the truth about the visit in order to show respect toward her husband. After getting off the bus, Rosa became frightened by the barbed wire fencing, the correctional officers with rifles and batons, and the security system. Maria's underlying ambivalent feelings about continuing the relationship seemed to be reflected through her daughter's behavior.

The prison counselor received permission to contact Maria's mental health therapist in order to coordinate counseling services between the facility and the community. In addition, he was able to connect Maria to a local self-help group for wives of inmates that provided transportation services and child care for children while parents visited at the facility. Maria also agreed to return to the facility for a joint session with Julio to clarify and resolve their relationship dilemma. In addition, Julio was seen individually by the prison counselor in order to identify his wishes for his children and his feelings about his relationship with his common-law wife.

Case Number 2: John and Denise Rockwell

John Rockwell is a thirty-seven-year-old white inmate who has recently come to the attention of the prison counselor. He was serving time in disciplinary detention for assault on other inmates and correctional officers. A predicate felon, he has served about half of a fifteen year sentence for second degree murder. His wife, Denise, cares for their three children and works as an administrative assistant in a large state agency. Since being employed she has been very successful and earns a good living. Early in her husband's sentence, Denise frequently visited her spouse. Two years ago they also began to have conjugal visits and have had six altogether.

Denise and their adolescent children live in comfortable surroundings in an apartment building. The past few times that John has called home, his children have been reporting to him that their mother has been out very late, saying that she is working. His wife has been rather distant on the phone and has not been responding to his frequent letters, saying she is too busy with work and the children to write, although she urges them to write. John's assaultive behavior has occurred immediately following incidents where he has been taunted by his tier mates who say that the word on the street is that his wife is having an affair. John's latest detention resulted from an assault on an inmate who made a suggestive remark about his wife.

During the counselor's first interview with John she learned that John was quite distraught and having thoughts of suicide because he felt so powerless about his marital situation. Just prior to this assault, John had been thinking that what he was hearing about his wife having an affair must be true since she was not at home as she had promised to receive his phone call. He also said that Denise was very distant emotionally and neglected to send him a card for his birthday. During the first session, the counselor helped John connect his thoughts of suicide, assaultive behavior, and depression to his deep feelings of hurt and abandonment. The counselor made a referral to the prison's mental health unit for an evaluation for possible medication.

During subsequent counseling sessions with John, the counselor helped him have better control over his rage through the use of anger management techniques and assertiveness training. The counselor also helped John to realize that he needed to discuss the issue of his wife's alleged affairs with her directly. In addition, she began to help John realize that although he could not control his wife's behavior, his own attitudes and behaviors were under his control and over the last couple of years he may have been responsible for some of his wife's emotional coolness. John was envious of her freedom, work success, and friendships. And he sometimes minimized her difficulties by not listening to her, changing the subject to his concerns, or demanding that she follow his "orders" about their children. In time, John was able to take more responsibility for his attitudes and behaviors toward not only his wife but also his fellow inmates and the correctional personnel. The counselor also helped John to set limits on his behavior through the use of confrontation, finding alternative ways of expressing anger, and role playing ways of dealing with situations on the tiers and with his wife.

As the counselor was able to gain John's trust, she also helped him to respond to his wife differently during phone contacts. During a conjugal visit, John was able to ask his wife about his suspicions of her having an affair without being defensive or emotionally assaultive. With some hesitation and fear, she was able to admit to her own need for male attention and affirmation. However, on the next visit, she asked John for a divorce, saying she had moved on in her life and was unwilling to wait until John was released. Although John became angry and then depressed, through individual grief work therapy and participation in a fathers-in-prison group he was able to ventilate his pain and sadness appropriately.

Case Number 3: Jerome and Lawonda Williams

Jerome Williams has been incarcerated in a prison facility that has a conjugal visiting program. His criminal activity surfaced after he began abusing drugs. His drug use began when he was in Vietnam as a noncommissioned officer who served for ten years in the Marine Corps. Although he had marketable employment skills, frequent layoffs at the automobile manufacturing company led to a revival of his drug and alcohol abuse.

Lawonda Williams frequently communicated with her husband Jerome by phone and in letters. She owns a home and has received much practical assistance from her parents, to whom she is very close emotionally; Jerome's family helps out as well. She works third shift as a licensed practical nurse in a local hospital. She has three older children, ages 20, 18, and 16, who are able to care for her youngest daughter, Christal, age 9, while she is at work. She regularly attends church services and her minister visits with her husband at the prison facility.

Initially, the conjugal visits went very smoothly, and the family enjoyed playing games and spending time with one another. Jerome enjoys his parenting role and is in recovery from his substance abuse, having entered a special program at the facility for drug and alcohol abuse. A Vietnam veterans group has helped him to get in touch with and express his sense of depersonalization during the war. However, Lawonda and Jerome rarely have sexual intercourse with one another during the visits, about which Jerome is extremely unhappy.

Through the help of her minister, Lawonda was able to speak frankly during a support group meeting for wives that was held after a conjugal visit. The group's facilitator obtained permission from Lawonda to speak to the family service program counselor at the prison. The counselor learned that Lawonda's refusal to have sexual intercourse with Jerome is related to her fear of possible HIV infection, since her husband is a former intravenous drug user. Although she is sure that her husband has remained faithful to her, she is also afraid that he may have had homosexual activity while in prison, which would also put him at risk of AIDS. As it turns out, Jerome had also spoken to the family services caseworker about his wife's reluctance to have sexual intercourse with him. Through a series of telephone contacts with Lawonda Williams and in-person contact with her husband, the counselor made plans for a conjoint therapy session.

With support from the counselor Lawonda was able to voice her concern about her fear of AIDS and encourage Jerome to be tested for the HIV virus. Although the counselor could not mandate that Jerome get tested, he supported Lawonda's request. Jerome honored his wife's request for his own sense of well-being and hers. He was also able to reassure her about not having sexual contact with other inmates while he was incarcerated.

Case Number 4: Jesus and Christina Ramone

Jesus Ramone and his wife, Christina, have been married for ten years. She has been living with her parents for the last three years. Christina's parents generally have been supportive of her efforts to visit her husband while he has been serving time in prison for the last seven years. For example, Christina's mother babysits for the children after school and on weekends. Jesus has earned his GED while in prison and plans to move into his father-in-law's home after his release, which should occur in about three months.

Although his prerelease furlough visits with his wife have been relatively smooth, Jesus has confided to the prison counselor, Father Ramarez, that he has been worried about being released from prison. He has been having difficulties finding a job and is not enthusiastic about living with his in-laws. Their home is small, and he is worried that his father-in-law will try to "push him around." Also, his father-in-law has developed a close relationship with Jesus' oldest son, Trini, which has made Jesus jealous. Jesus has been reluctant to discuss his concerns with his wife and in-laws.

Father Ramarez suggested to Jesus that he might be able to be helpful to him by having some family counseling sessions with his wife and at some point with his in-laws. While on a home visit, Jesus asked his wife to join him and Father Ramarez in some counseling at the prison facility. Jesus told his wife that he was concerned about moving back home and finding a job to support the family. He further stated to her that his manliness and "being back in charge of the family" was very important to him.

During several counseling sessions, Father Ramarez helped Jesus and Christina learn about one another's concerns and the changes that have occurred during their separation from one another. Jesus learned about his wife's difficulties with maintaining the family without her husband. Jesus further understood that without Christina's father's help when he was first arrested and imprisoned, Trini's initial behavior problems at home, minor altercations with the law, and problems at school might have gotten out of hand.

Jesus admitted to his wife that he was worried about leaving prison and returning home. He had become a leader in the prison's Latino community and would miss the status he was accorded in that role. He was frightened about his future on the outside. Even though his father-in-law had offered him an automobile mechanic's job, Jesus was fearful of "not being his own man" in the eyes of his family.

Father Ramarez, counseling within a cultural context and understanding the changes occurring within the family over time, was able to help the Ramones understand one another and approach their reunion cautiously but optimistically. A three-way meeting between Jesus, his father-in-law, and Trini took place to talk about the grandfather's, father's, and the son's relationships with one another. Jesus and his father-in-law also discussed the possibility of a job and Jesus' desire to also seek out other possibilities. Father Ramarez's suggestion that the Chicano Family Service Agency could continue to assist the family after Jesus' release was accepted by all concerned. Father Ramarez and the parole officer worked together during this transition period from prison to the community and a strong link to the community counseling agency was made for the Ramone family.

SUMMARY

This chapter has discussed issues of concern to those wishing to perform clinical roles in correctional facilities. An ecological perspective is recommended for understanding the family-related problems of inmates as they are manifested in the complex, security-conscious environment of the correctional facility. Thus, to be effective, counselors and caseworkers must be aware of these complexities and attend to these concerns.

Correctional counselors need a variety of therapeutic skills and techniques, expertise in case management, and the ability to link with other professionals within the prison setting and with community agencies. Because individuals from ethnic minority groups are overrepresented in the prison population, counselors must also be knowledgeable about ethnic and racial diversity. Finally, counselors need to be aware of their own biases and of inmate reactions to their helping efforts.

Inmates and their families often have a multitude of problems, and the counselor must be able to evaluate the strengths and weaknesses of each inmate and family. At different points within the criminal justice process, inmates and families may be especially vulnerable to particular problems and have specific needs. Prior difficulties that have been left unresolved may become exacerbated during particular stages of the criminal justice process.

One strategy to help gain inmate trust may be through involvement of family members and other sources of social support in the counseling process. During traditional visits, furloughs, and conjugal visits, couple and family counseling sessions may be useful in helping inmates maintain or strengthen relationships with their families. Case examples of how clinical interventions can assist in this process were used illustratively.

NOTE

1. More information can be obtained from the authors at Family ReEntry, 60 Roton Avenue, Norwalk, CT 05853.

Chapter 9

Conclusions and Research Recommendations

This final chapter has two goals: to summarize the salient findings of the research, bearing in mind its limitations, and to offer suggestions for future research on inmate family relationships.

CONCLUSIONS

Conducting research on an incarcerated population is difficult. Among other problems, there are few incentives that can be offered for participation and little reason for inmates or facility staff to comply with the research agenda. In the case of wives of inmates, there are myriad practical problems as well. In addition, participation in this research necessitated that a vulnerable population trust the investigators sufficiently to share their thoughts and feelings about a difficult and painful part of their lives.

As a result, the sample studied was relatively small and of unknown representativeness in terms of the overall population of married inmates and their wives. However, despite these problems, the congruence of our findings with those of other scholars suggests that the inmates and wives studied here are reasonably typical of the larger population of married inmates and their wives, although one must be cautious in generalizing the findings.

As expected, we found that incarceration is a very stressful experience for inmates and their families. Despite the level of stress reported, both inmates and wives were found to be coping extremely well when compared with norms from a standardized coping measure developed on a more representative cross section of families. The participants did particularly well in their use of cognitive means of coping (the family appraisal or "C" factor in Hill's model), which enables them to define stressful events in ways that make them more manageable and to accept this difficult situation with a minimum of reactivity. Interestingly, there were few ethnic differences in coping; most striking was the similarity in coping across gender and ethnic groups.

Another important coping strategy for these couples was communication with one another by telephone, letters, and face-to-face visits. However, these forms of communication were rated more positively by the inmates than their wives, as reflected in higher coping scores by inmates who reported more frequent contact with their spouses. It is unclear why these forms of communication were not evaluated more positively by wives, although it may be related to the higher costs of maintaining communication for wives, both financially and in terms of their time, as compared to their husbands.

Consistent with the literature, wives were found to receive both practical and emotional support from their own families, and to a lesser extent from the inmate's family. However, there was widespread sentiment that this support was insufficient to meet their needs. These unmet needs have implications for services offered by community agencies.

Also remarkable is the finding that inmates and wives have emotionally close, cohesive relationships despite the separation caused by incarceration. On the other hand, problems were evident in the adaptability of these marriages, manifested in issues of marital leadership, roles, and relationship rules. These problems are perhaps expectable based on the life circumstances in which these families find themselves, where there is genuine confusion about who is in charge, what the rules should be, and who is performing which family roles. This is reflected in the shift reported in decision making between the preincarceration period and the time of the study, where husbands became less influential and wives became more influential. But despite not living at home, most inmates retained some control over decision making, especially over some child-related and economic decisions. Again, one is more impressed by the similarities in findings across ethnic groups than the differences.

Another important conclusion pertains to the importance accorded by these inmates to the father role, again consistent with findings from the few research studies investigating this issue. The inmates studied here placed high importance on their roles as fathers and felt emotionally close to their children despite not playing a part in their day-to-day lives. This has important implications for the future insofar as most of these offenders will return to the community and resume their roles as fathers. In fact, because of their stigmatized and societally devalued status as criminal offenders, the role of father is one of the few roles that they can look forward to assuming successfully upon release. However, what correctional systems do (or fail to do) to support and encourage family roles will be critically important in influencing the quality of father-child relationships that are available to these men. Clearly, it is in society's best interest, as well as that of the inmate and his family, to invest resources into nurturing these relationships so that they do not deteriorate over time.

One way of nurturing father-child relationships is through extended family visit programs such as New York State's Family Reunion Program (FRP). This program enables participating inmates and their families to experience in a limited way some of the normal aspects of family life that they sorely miss as a consequence of incarceration. These include talking and eating together, playing games and watching TV, and being able to express physical affection.

It was disappointing to find that participation in the FRP was unrelated to most aspects of marital functioning studied here, including emotional closeness, cohesion, adaptability, coping, and most types of decision making. This may be a function of the high variability that occurred in the number of visits experienced by the total group, as well as the length of time over which the visits occurred. It may be that for such visits to be reflected in the quality of marital relations they must occur more frequently or over a long period of time. Another suggestion might be to strongly encourage marital or family counseling in conjunction with visits, to help participants use the occasion of the visit more constructively.

On the other hand, when participants were asked about feelings of closeness to one another after participation in FRP visits in contrast to before they started, there was strong agreement that closeness increased following visits. Unfortunately, FRP visits appear to be viewed more positively by the inmates than their wives. This may be understandable insofar as wives bear the responsibility for visit preparation and transportation to the facility.

RESEARCH RECOMMENDATIONS

In some ways this research has raised as many questions as it has answered. While valuable knowledge has been obtained regarding inmate family relationships, much more must be learned if we are to effectively use the rehabilitation potential of families on behalf of inmates. In general, much more research is needed on inmate fathers, focused first, on their feelings and attitudes about fatherhood and their children, and second, on the nature of their relationships with their children and the factors that affect those ties.

The following specific hypotheses are generated for future research on inmate family relationships:

1. More intensive inmate-wife communication is associated with healthier marriages.
2. Healthier marriages are associated with better inmate adjustment to prison life.
3. Marriages with preexisting problems are more vulnerable to divorce in response to incarceration.
4. Children who have closer relationships with their fathers exhibit fewer problems during their father's incarceration.

5. Children who are told the truth about where their father is and why exhibit fewer problems during their father's incarceration.

In addition, several questions are posed to guide future research. These include:

1. Why do some marriages get stronger during incarceration whereas others break down?
2. Where there is a poor marital relationship between the inmate and his wife, can early intervention help preserve the marriage?
3. Does marital counseling in conjunction with FRP visits lead to stronger, more resilient marriages?

References

Angell, R. C. (1936). *The Family Encounters the Depression.* New York: Scribner.

Bakker, L. J., Morris, B. A., and Janus, L. M. (1978). Hidden victims of crime. *Social Work,* 23, 143–178.

Balogh, T. K. (1964). Conjugal visiting in prisons: A sociological perspective. *Federal Probation,* 28 (Sept.), 52–58.

Bauhofer, V. (1987). Prison parenting: A challenge for children's advocates. *Children Today,* 16 (1), 15–16.

Bennett, L. A. (1989). Current views of inmate visiting. In *Voices and Visions: The Family and Corrections.* Proceedings of the First National Conference on Family and Corrections. April 24–27, 1988, Sacramento, CA, 25–27.

Boszonmanyi-Nagy and Spark, G. M. (1973). *Invisible Loyalties: Reciprocity in Intergenerational Family Therapy.* New York: Harper and Row.

Boudouris, J. (1985). *Prisons and Kids: Programs for Inmate Parents.* College Park, MD: American Correctional Association.

Boyd-Franklin, N. (1989). *Black Families in Therapy: A Multisystems Approach.* New York: Guilford Press.

Brodsky, N. (1975). *Family and Friends of Men in Prison.* Lexington, MA: Lexington Books.

Burr, W. R. (1973). *Theory Construction and the Sociology of the Family.* New York: Wiley.

Burstein, J. Q. (1977). *Conjugal Visits in Prison.* Lexington, MA: Lexington Books.

Bush, E. L. (1990). Defandants' children at sentencing. *Federal Probation,* 54, 15–21.

Cavan, R. S. and Zemans E. (1958). Marital relationships of prisoners in twenty-eight countries. *Journal of Criminal Law, Criminology and Police Science*, 49, 133–139.

Chaiklin, H. (1972). Integrating correctional and family systems. *American Journal of Orthopsychiatry*, 42, 784–791.

Cobean, S. and Power, P. W. (1978). The role of the family in the rehabilitation of the offender. *International Journal of Offender Therapy and Comparative Criminology*, 22, 29–38.

Couturier, L. and Cohen, H. (1991). The incarcerated fathers group. *Family and Corrections Network News*, 3, 5–7.

Crosthwaite, A. (1972). Voluntary work with families of prisoners. *International Journal of Offender Therapy and Comparative Criminology*, 16, 253–259.

Crosthwaite, A. (1975). Punishment for whom? The prisoner or his wife? *International Journal of Offender Therapy and Comparative Criminology*, 19, 275–285.

Daniel, S. W. and Barrett, C. J. (1981). The needs of prisoners' wives: A challenge for mental health professionals. *Community Mental Health Journal*, 7, 310–322.

Drug programs sought for inmates. (1990, May 2). *The Times Union*, p. A-2.

Duffee, D. E. (1989). *Corrections Practice and Policy*. New York: Random House.

Ekland-Olson, S., Supancic, M., Campbell, J., and Lenihan, K. J. (1983). Postrelease depression and the importance of familial support. *Criminology*, 21, 253–275.

Family Reunion Program. (1980). Directive #4500, Albany, NY: New York State Department of Correctional Services.

Fenlon, M. (1972). An innovative project for wives and families of prisoners. *F.C.I. Treatment Notes*, 3, 1–12.

Fenton, N. (1959). *The Prisoner's Family: A Study of Family Counseling in an Adult Correctional Setting*. Palo Alto: Pacific Books.

Fishman, L. T. (1990). *Women at the Wall: A Study of Prisoners' Wives Doing Time on the Outside*. Albany, New York: State University of New York Press.

Fishman, S. (1983). The impact of incarceration on children of offenders. *Journal of Children in Contemporary Society*, 15, 89–99.

Fishman, S. H. (1981). Losing a loved one to incarceration: The effect of imprisonment on family members. *The Personnel and Guidance Journal*, 59(6), 372–375.

Fishman, S. H. and Alissi, A. (1979). Strengthening families as natural support systems for offenders. *Federal Probation*, 43 (Sept.), 16–21.

Flanagan, T. J. (1981). Dealing with long-term confinement: Adaptive strategies and perspectives among long-term prisoners. *Criminal Justice and Behavior*, 8, 201–222.

Flanagan, T. J. and Maguire, K. (1990). *Sourcebook on criminal justice statistics—1989*. U.S. Department of Justice, Bureau of Justice Statistics. Washington, D.C.: USGPO.

Fox, G. L. (1981). The family and the ex-offender: Potential for rehabilitation. In S. Martin et al. (Eds.), *New Directions in the Rehabilitation of Criminal Offenders*. Washington, D.C.: National Academy Press.

Freedman, B. J. and Rice, D. G. (1977). Marital therapy in prison: One-partner "couple therapy." *Federal Probation*, 40, 175–183.

Friedman, S. and Esselstyn, T. C. (1965). The adjustment of children of jail inmates. *Federal Probation*, 29, 55–59.

Fritsch, T. A. and Burkhead, J. D. (1981). Behavioral reactions of children to parental absence due to imprisonment. *Family Relations*, 30, 83–88.

Garland, D. (1990). *Punishment and Modern Society: A Study in Social Theory*. Chicago, IL: University of Chicago Press.

Gaudin, J. M. (1984). Social work role and tasks with incarcerated mothers. *Social Casework*, 65, 279–286.

Gelman, S. R. (1983). Correctional Policies: Evolving trends. In A. R. Roberts (Ed.), *Social Work in Juvenile and Criminal Justice Settings* (pp. 45–65). Springfield, IL: C. C. Thomas.

Glaser, N. (1964). *The Effectiveness of a Prison and Parole System*. New York: Bobbs-Merrill.

Goetting, A. (1982). Conjugal association in prison: The debate and its resolutions. *New England Journal on Prison Law*, 8, 141–154.

Gottfredson, S. D. and McConville, S. (1987). Introduction. In S. D. Gottfredson and S. McConville (Eds.), *America's Correctional Crisis: Prison Populations and Public Policy* (pp. 3–11). New York: Greenwood Press.

Gottfredson, S. D. and Taylor, R. B. (1987). Attitudes of correctional policymakers and the public. In S. D. Gottfredson and S. McConville (Eds.), *America's Correctional Crisis: Prison Populations and Public Policy* (pp. 57–75). New York: Greenwood Press.

Hairston, C. F. (1988). Family ties during imprisonment: Do they influence future criminal activity? *Federal Probation*, 52, 48–52.

Hairston, C. F. (1990). Men in prison: Family characteristics and parenting views. *Journal of Offender Counseling, Services and Rehabilitation*, 14, 23–30.

Hairston, C. F. and Hess, P. M. (1986). Regulating parent-child communication in correctional settings. *Proceedings of the First National Conference on Family and Corrections*. Waynesboro, VA: Family and Corrections Network, pp. 29–32.

Hairston, C. F. and Lockett, P. W. (1987). Parents in prison: New directions for social services. *Social Work*, 32, 162–164.

Haley, J. (1973). *Uncommon Therapy: The Psychiatric Techniques of Milton H. Erickson, M.D.* New York: Norton.

Handler, E. (1975). Social work and corrections: Comments on an uneasy partnership. *Criminology*, 13(2), 240–254.

Hannon, G., Martin, D., and Martin, M. (1984). Incarceration in the family: Adjustment to change. *Family Therapy*, 11(3), 253–260.

Hansen, D. and Hill, R. (1964). Families under stress. In Christiansen, (Ed.), *Handbook of Marriage and the Family* (pp. 782–819). Chicago: Rand McNally.

Hatcher, H. (1978). *Correctional Casework and Counseling*. Englewood Cliffs, NJ: Prentice-Hall.

Haynor, N. S. (1972). Attitudes toward conjugal visits for prisoners. *Federal Probation*, 36, 43–49.

Hill, R. (1965). Generic features of families under stress. In H. J. Parad (Ed.), *Crisis Intervention: Selected Readings* (pp. 32–52). New York: Family Service Association of America.

Hill, R. (1972). *Strengths of Black Families*. New York: Emerson-Hall.

Hinds, L. (1981). Impact of incarceration on low-income families. *Journal of Offender Counseling, Services and Rehabilitation*, 5, 8–9.

Holt, N. and Miller, D. (1972). *Explorations in Inmate-Family Relationships*. Sacramento, CA: California Department of Corrections.

Homer, E. L. (1979). Inmate-family ties: Desirable but difficult. *Federal Probation*, 33 (March), 47–52.

Hopper, C. (1967). Conjugal visiting: A controversial practice in Mississippi. *Criminal Law Bulletin*, 3, 288–289.

Horton, H. and Wright, A. (1976). Visiting Dartmoor: Help for prisoners' families. *Prison Service Journal*, 12, 6–7.

Howlett, J. (1973). Marital deprivations of prisoners and their wives. *Prison Service Journal*, 23, 2–5.

Howser, J. F. and MacDonald, D. (1982). Maintaining family ties. *Corrections Today*, 44, 96–98.

Howser, J. E., Grossman, J., and MacDonald, D. (1983). Impact of Family Reunion Program on institutional discipline. *Journal of Offender Counseling, Services and Rehabilitation*, 8, 27–36.

Hughes, J. E. (1982). "My daddy's number is C-92760." *Journal of Children in Contemporary Society*, 15, 79–87.

Ingram, G. and Swartzfager, A. (1973). Involving families and the community in rehabilitating offenders. *Hospital and Community Psychiatry*, 24, 616–618.

Inmate growth doubled in 1980s. (1990, January 26). *The Times Union*, p. A-4.

Inmate population rises 134% over last decade (1991, May 16). *The Times Union*, p. A-1, A-12.

Inmate population sets record (1990, May 2). *The Times Union*, p. A-2.

Jamieson, K. M. and Flanagan, T. J. (1989). *Sourcebook of Criminal Justice Statistics—1988*. U.S. Department of Justice, Bureau of Justice Statistics. Washington, D.C.: USGPO.

Johns, D. (1971). Alternatives to conjugal visiting. *Federal Probation*, 35 (March), 48–52.

Jorgensen, J. D., Hernandez, S. H., and Warren, R. C. (1986). Addressing the social needs of families of prisoners: A tool for inmate rehabilitation. *Federal Probation*, 50, 47–52.

Kaslow, F. W. (1978). Marital and family therapy for prisoners and their spouses and families. *Prison Journal*, 58, 53–59.

Kiersh, E. (1979). A private California agency tries to keep prisoners and their families together. *Corrections Magazine*, 5.

Killinger, G., Cromwell, P. F., and Wood, J. (1979). *Penology: The Evolution of Corrections in America*. St. Paul, MN: West Publishing.

Kiser, G. C. (1991). Female inmates and their families. *Federal Probation*, 55, 56–63.

Lanier, C. S. (1987). *Fathers in Prison: A Psychosocial Exploration.* Paper presented at the Annual Meeting of the American Society of Criminology, Montreal, Canada.

Lanier, C. S. (1989). First father's day event. *Family and Corrections Network News*, 2, 3.

Leclair, D. P. (1978). Home furlough program effects on rates of recidivism. *Criminal Justice and Behavior*, 5, 249–259.

London, H. and Devore, W. (1988). Layers of understanding: Counseling ethnic minority families. *Family Relations*, 37, 310–314.

Lowenstein, A. (1984). Coping with stress: The case of prisoners' wives. *Journal of Marriage and the Family*, 46, 699–708.

Lowenstein, A. (1986). Temporary single parenthood—The case of prisoners' families. *Family Relations*, 35, 79–95.

Malcolm, A. H. (1990, October 10). New strategies to fight crime go far beyond stiffer terms and more cells. *The New York Times*, p. A16.

Markley, C. (1973). Furlough programs and conjugal visiting in adult correctional institutions. *Federal Probation*, 37, 19–26.

Marlette, M. (1990). Furloughs tightened—Success rates high. *Corrections Compendium*, 15(1), 6–21.

Marsh, R. L. (1983). Services for families: A model project to provide services for families of prisoners. *International Journal of Offender Therapy and Comparative Criminology*, 27, 156–162.

Martinson, R. (1974). What works?—Questions and answers about prison reform. *Public Interest*, 35, 22–54.

McCubbin, H. I. (1979). Integrating coping behavior in family stress theory. *Journal of Marriage and the Family*, 41, 237–244.

McCubbin, H. I., Larsen, A., and Olson, D. H. (1981). *F-COPES: Family Crisis Oriented Personal Evaluation Scales*. St. Paul, MN: Family Social Sciences, University of Minnesota.

McCubbin, M. A. and McCubbin, H. I. (1987). Family stress theory and measurement: The T-Double ABCX Model of family adjustment and adaptation. In H. I. McCubbin and A. I. Thompson (Eds.), *Family Assessment Inventories for Research and Practice* (pp. 3–32). Madison, WI: Family Stress Coping and Health Project.

McGahey, R. (1988). Corrections and criminal justice. In J. L. Mumpower and W. L. Ilchman (Eds), *New York State in the Year 2000* (pp. 525–559). Albany, New York: State University of New York Press.

Minuchin, S. (1974). *Families and Family Therapy*. Cambridge, MA: Harvard University Press.

Moerk, E. (1973). Like father like son: Imprisonment of fathers and the psychological adjustment of sons. *Journal of Youth and Adolescence*, 2, 4.

Morris, P. (1965). *Prisoner Family Relationships*. New York: Hart.

Morris, P. (1967). Fathers in prison. *British Journal of Criminology*, 7, 424–430.

Nagel, W. (1973). *The New Red Barn: A Critical Look at the Modern American Prison*. New York: Walker.

Netherland, W. (1987). Correctional system: Adult. In A. Minahan (Ed.), *Encyclopedia of Social Work* (18th ed.) (pp. 351–360). Silver Spring, MD: National Association of Social Workers.

O'Block, R. L. (1986). *Criminal Justice Research Sources*. Cincinnati, OH: Anderson Publishing Co.

Olson, D. H., Portner, J., and Lavee, Y. (1985). *FACES III*. St. Paul, MN: Family Social Science, University of Minnesota.

Public/Private Ventures. (1990). Serving unwed teen fathers: A new demonstration. *Public/Private Venture*, 15, 1.

Pueschel, J. and Moglia, R. (1977). The effects of the penal environment on familial relationships. *Family Coordinator*, 26, 373–375.

Rieger, W. (1973). A proposal for a trial of family therapy and conjugal visits in prison. *American Journal of Orthopsychiatry*, 43, 117–122.

Roberts, A. R. (1983). *Social Work in Juvenile and Criminal Justice Settings*. Springfield, IL: C. C. Thomas.

Rogers, J. W. (1989). The greatest correctional myth: Winning the war on crime through incarceration. *Federal Probation*, 53, 21–28.

Rosenfeld, J. M., Rosenstein, E., and Raab, M. (1973). Sailor families: The nature and effects of one kind of father absence. *Child Welfare*, 52, 33–44.

Rothman, D. J. (1971). *The Discovery of the Asylum*. Boston: Little Brown.

Sack, W. H. (1977). Children of imprisoned fathers. *Psychiatry*, 40, 163–174.

Sack, W. H., Seidler, J., and Thomas, S. (1976). The children of imprisoned parents: A psychosocial exploration. *American Journal of Orthopsychiatry*, 46, 618–628.

Sanchez-Ayendez, M. (1988). The Puerto Rican American family. In C. H. Mindell, R. W. Haberstein, and R. Wright (Eds.), *Ethnic Families in America* (pp. 173–195). New York: Elsevier.

Schafer, N. E. (1977). Prisoner visiting—A background for change. *Federal Probation*, 42 (Sept.), 47–50.

Schneller, D. P. (1975a). Some social and psychological effects of incarceration on the families of Negro prisoners. *American Journal of Corrections*, 37, 29–33.

Schneller, D. P. (1975b). Prisoners' families: A study of some social and psychological effects of incarceration on the families of Negro prisoners. *Criminology*, 14, 402–412.

Schneller, D. P. (1976). *The Prisoner's Family: A Study of the Effects of Imprisonment on the Families of Prisoners*. San Francisco: Rand E. Research Associates.

Schneller, D. P. (1990). Criminal rehabilitation: The role of the family. *Family and Corrections Network News*, 2(1), 6–8.

Schwartz, M. C. and Weintraub, J. F. (1974). The prisoner's wife: A study in crisis. *Federal Probation*, 38, 20–27.

Scott, J. (1983). The forgotten family. *Journal of Offender Counseling*, 3, 34–39.

Selsky, C. S. (1962). Post-commitment family counseling. *Federal Probation*, 26, 41–43.

Sherman, M., and Hawkins, G. (1981). *Imprisonment in America: Choosing the Future*. Chicago: University of Chicago Press.

Showalter, D. and Hunsinger, M. (1985). Social work in a maximum security setting. In A. R. Roberts (Ed.), *Social Work in Juvenile and Criminal Justice Settings* (pp. 257–275). Springfield, IL: C. C. Thomas.

Showalter, D. and Jones, C. W. (1980). Marital and family counseling in prisons. *Social Work*, 25, 224–228.

Solomon, B. (1979). *Black Empowerment*. New York: Columbia University Press.

Spiro, B. (1978). The future course of corrections. *Social Work*, 23, 315–320.

Swan, A. L. (1981). *Families of Black Prisoners*. Boston: G. K. Hall and Co.

Thomas, C. (1990, May 17). Michigan puts a stop to building of new prisons. *The Times Union*, p. A-15.

Thomas, R. G. (1981). The family practitioner and the criminal justice system: Challenges for the 80's. *Family Relations*, 30, 614–624.

Thompson, J. W. (1984). Crisis intervention with prisoners and their children. *Emotional First Aid: A Journal of Crisis Intervention*, 1, 5–16.

U.S. has highest rate of imprisonment in the world. (1991, January 7). *The New York Times*, p. A14.

Weintraub, J. F. (1976). The delivery of services to families of prisoners. *Federal Probation*, 40, 28–31.

Wilmer, H. M., Marks, I., and Pogue, E. (1966). Group treatment of prisoners and their families. *Mental Hygiene*, 50, 380–389.

Zemans, E. and Cavan, R. S. (1958). Marital relationships of prisoners. *Journal of Criminal Law and Police Science*, 49, 50–57.

Index

Fritsch, Travis A., 32
FRP. *See* Family Reunion Program
Furloughs, 38, 40–42, 105, 109

Garland, David, 4
Gaudin, James M., 32, 125
Gelman, Sheldon R., 2, 3, 5
Glaser, Nathan, 15, 42
Goetting, Ann, 38, 39, 40, 42
Gottfredson, Stephen D., 1, 5, 7, 10, 11
Grief, 26, 31, 130

Hairston, Creasie F., 9, 26, 34, 37, 84, 103, 110, 115, 116
Haley, Jay, 132
Handler, Ellen, 2, 5, 124, 125
Hannon, Ginger, 22, 23, 25, 26, 78
Hansen, Donald, 19, 20, 72
Hatcher, Hayes, 4
Hawkins, Gordon, 4
Haynor, Norman S., 39
Hess, Peg M., 37, 116
Hill, Robert, 63, 65
Hill, Rubin, 15, 16, 17, 20, 21, 24, 55, 72
Hinds, Lennox, 15, 24, 29, 30
History, of corrections, 3–4
Holt, Norman, 23, 27, 42, 43, 78, 107, 108, 110
Hopper, Columbus, 38
Horton, Helen, 120
Howlett, J., 23, 26, 28, 29
Howser, James F., 26, 38, 39, 42, 48, 102, 109
Hughes, James E., 31

Hunsinger, Marian, 11, 23, 25, 126, 131

Incarceration, rates, 1–2, 7–8
Ingram, Gilbert, 15, 22, 101, 120
Intervention, 6, 123–42

Jamieson, Katherine M., 8, 9, 10, 11, 50, 126
Johns, Donald, 40, 41
Jones, Charlotte W., 12, 24, 27, 32, 77, 127, 130, 131, 132, 133
Jorgensen, James D., 2, 23, 104, 107, 110, 125

Kaslow, Florence W., 36, 110, 118, 119, 131, 132, 133
Kiersh, Ed, 12, 121
Kiser, George C., 15, 30

Lanier, Charles S., 25, 84, 114, 116
Leclair, Daniel P., 41
Lockett, Patricia W., 110, 115
London, Harlon, 62, 64
Lowenstein, Ariela, 32, 34, 35

MacDonald, Donald, 26, 39, 42, 48, 102, 109
Maguire, Kathleen, 7, 8, 9
Malcolm, Andrew H., 10
Marital relationships, 23–24, 46, 75–78, 101, 111
Markley, Carson, 41
Marlette, Marjorie, 41
Marriage, 9, 13, 27, 69
Marsh, Robert L., 23, 114
Martinson, Robert, 6

About the Authors

BONNIE E. CARLSON is Associate Professor in the School of Social Work, State University of New York at Albany. She is an editor of *No Child Is Unadoptable: Reader on the Adoption of Children with Special Needs* (1980) and has written and conducted research on domestic violence, social work with vulnerable groups, and drug addiction.

NEIL CERVERA, Clinical Assistant Professor, Albany Medical College, and Assistant Professor, School of Social Work, State University of New York at Albany, has written on family support programs, teenage pregnancy, and involuntary childlessness.